PEMBROKESHIRE'S
FORTS & MILITARY AIRFIELDS
1535-2010

PEMBROKESHIRE'S
FORTS & MILITARY AIRFIELDS
1535-2010

by

BENJAMIN A. PHILLIPS

LOGASTON PRESS

LOGASTON PRESS
Little Logaston, Logaston,
Woonton, Almeley, Herefordshire HR3 6QH
www.logastonpress.co.uk

Published by Logaston Press 2013
Copyright © text Benjamin A. Phillips 2013
Copyright © illustrations as acknowledged

ISBN 978 1 906663 73 5

Typeset by Logaston Press
and printed and bound in Poland
www.polskabook.pl

Contents

Acknowledgements

The author would like to extend a special thanks to the following for their contributions and photographs; Airfield Research Group, Air Heritage (Wales), Prof. Benjamin Owens, *Brawdy Stronghold in the West* (History Press), CADW, *Castles and Fortifications of Wales* (Amberley), Coflein, *Defending Wales* (Amberley), Deric Brock, *Discovering Fortifications* (Shire Books), Fleet Air Arm Museum, Guntower Museum at Pembroke Dock, Haverfordwest Museum, Imperial War Museum at London, Landmark Trust, Pembrokeshire Libraries, *Military Airfields of Wales* (Bridge Books), Military Heritage of Pembrokeshire, Naval History Homepage, National Maritime Museum, Palmerston Forts Society, Pembrokeshire Coast Photographs, Planed, Royal Armouries in Leeds, Royal Commission on Ancient and Historical Monuments Wales (RCHAMW), Scolton Museum, Subbrit, Swansea Museum, Tenby Museum, Texaco Ltd., and the Welsh Assembly Government (Photographic Archives).

1   Introduction

Much has been written about the medieval castles of Pembrokeshire and their decline, but historians have given much less attention to the fortifications that were built around the county's coast in the age of artillery and the time of the steam warships of the 18th and 19th centuries. This book traces the history and development of fortifications around the Pembrokeshire coast from the reign of Henry VIII to recent times. Castles had been built before artillery was even a concept, and its arrival led to attempts to adapt castles to equip themselves with the new weapon, and defend themselves against the attacks of others. Castle walls were vulnerable to an attacker's artillery bombardment; they were easily knocked down, and the shattering stonework often endangered the defenders rather than protecting them. A new style of defensive structure was required, and Henry VIII came up with a unique castle and blockhouse design, concentrating on artillery defence. In the following years the fort was further developed to include all the designs seen today.

From the point of view of defending itself, Great Britain is fortunate to be an island. From Henry VIII's reign, a line of forts and fortified gun batteries were located at intervals along the south coast, and these, with the sea acting as a natural moat, have been an ideal barrier against invasion. Gradually the need for such protection extended to other parts of the coastline including Pembrokeshire, and particularly the Milford Haven waterway. These new forts were often hurriedly built and took up a vast amount of the nation's finance, materials and manpower, and in most cases their armament was obsolete before they were declared operational and they had to be re-armed at additional cost. As we shall see, some forts that were built, such as Scoveston in Pembrokeshire, had no real purpose as the area was already covered by other forts.

In addition to forts, several gun batteries were also built. These cost a fraction of the expense of building a fort, but they were effective. The guns were well protected in casements, and the batteries included all the necessary ancillary buildings such as magazines and quarters for the garrison.

In a Royal Commission report of 1860 on the defence of the United Kingdom, three areas in Wales were identified as being at potential risk of invasion. The main concern was Milford Haven in Pembrokeshire, and several forts and batteries were built to protect the waterway with its sheltered anchorage and the royal dockyard at Pembroke Dock. The second area was around the southern coast of Pembrokeshire, which, with its sandy beaches and sheltered bays, was a likely target for a seaborne invasion. The third area deemed to need protection was the Welsh coast of the Bristol Channel and the industrial ports of south Wales.

Most of the fortifications built soon became obsolete due to the development of iron-clad ships and the armament that they could carry, and came to be known as Palmerston's Follies (as it was Lord Palmerston who had the forts constructed). Re-arming forts was rarely seen as a priority and when carried out only a modest budget was allocated for the purpose even when, for example, the Stanhope Committee of 1904 recommended that certain fortifications in Milford Haven should be equipped with the most modern guns available. Some of the fortifications were manned until the early 20th century, including the period of the First World War.

The whole nature of warfare changed during the Second World War as the German Blitzkrieg pushed through Europe at an alarming speed. Throughout Pembrokeshire new gun emplacements appeared, armed with a variety of dual-purpose artillery (both for surface action and against aircraft). The demands of the war necessitated the construction of a new type of structure: the military airfields whose mark on the landscape is most noticeable today. Their concrete and tarmac runways, together with the associated hangars, towers and other buildings, became the castles or forts of the 20th century. During the war, Pembrokeshire was to become a sort of aircraft carrier, with at least nine operational airfields.

Fortifications in the country and in Pembrokeshire have considerably changed over the centuries. Each type has played a part in defending the nation against many aggressors, from King Philip II of Spain, Louis XIV, and Napoleon Bonaparte to Kaiser Wilhelm II and Adolf Hitler.

2   From Castles to Forts

Castles belonged to the medieval era of overlordship and feudalism, while the later artillery forts emerged in the era of steam, the industrial revolution and more deadly and destructive weapons of war. But the concept and even the term 'fort' was nothing new. The early Iron Age settlements were protected by an enclosure referred to as a fort, at least subsequently. The Romans brought with them another fort design incorporating wooden towers and stone walls. They also introduced the idea of a water-filled ditch and other obstacles around the fort.

After the Roman armies left Britain in 410 AD, the country was left in a vacuum – a period of some 500 years that became known as the Dark Ages. Initially the Romanised areas in the vicinity of their towns and fortresses remained unchanged, following a way of life based on the Roman model. In time the Welsh people reclaimed their true identity and culture, with local chieftains reclaiming their inherited territory and establishing a simple form of protection for their people.

Meanwhile in England the Saxons settled and brought with them the 'burgh', a timbered wall and ditch surrounding a settlement. The arrival of the Normans brought the motte and bailey design – an earthen mound on which a tower was built, initially of timber for both speed of construction and to allow the mound time to stabilise before it was expected to carry a stone structure. From this would spread out a less well protected bailey, probably surrounded by a simple wooden stockade, in which buildings were erected to house retainers and stores. Over the decades, some castles were either gradually rebuilt and possibly extended, using stone, whilst others, no longer having a purpose, were left to decay.

Whilst castles were often built in towns, or to encourage the formation of towns, over which they exerted control and gave some protection,

*An artist's impression of Henry VIII's East Blockhouse at Angle,
shows how many of his structures would have originally looked.
The one at Angle has now largely fallen into the sea.*

the later artillery forts were built to protect ports and other important installations, together with sea lanes and sheltered anchorages for shipping. Aspects of their construction were derived from the castle, with, for example, the use of ditches, guarded gate houses and drawbridges.

A spur to the development of the artillery forts came during the reign of Henry VIII. When Henry broke with the Church of Rome, the pope encouraged Catholic nations to invade England. The king strengthened his navy and built a number of new fortifications known as blockhouses – round towers which could house large calibre cannons on the roof and in several embrasures; additional cannons could be placed in areas created in the vicinity of the tower often protected by a wall or earth embankment. Two were built to protect Milford Haven. This basic design remained unchanged for the next few centuries.

Castles in England and Wales were put to their ultimate test during the English Civil War, when they were assailed by gunpowder and cannon ball. Modifications were made, including enlarging arrow slits to take muskets and hand-held cannons, and ramps constructed against the inside of the outer walls on which to position larger field guns. Initially the castles were able to withstand assault and long sieges, but as the war continued it gave an impetus to the design of artillery, including the crea-

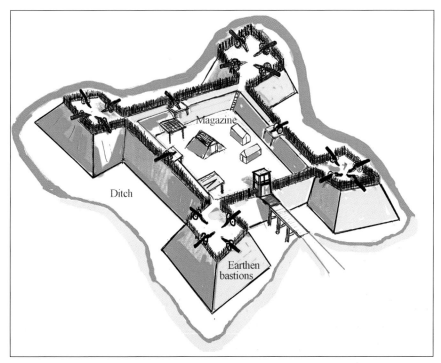

Drawing of an English Civil War sconce (fort).
The fort at Pill was of similar construction.

tion of heavier weapons. A 24-pounder light artillery gun could demolish a stone wall, so at least 15 feet of earth behind the wall was required to absorb the impact of the iron shot. Larger cannon were obviously capable of causing greater and more devastating damage. Castle walls were a clear target for these weapons which had a range of over a mile, and because existing castles often had limited space in which to shore up the stone walls with the necessary earth, occupiers soon began constructing defences some distance from the castles with additional ditches, ramparts and their own artillery positions.

One type of fort that appeared during the Civil War was the 'sconce', a small temporary earthwork and timber artillery fortification. These forts were star-shaped, with four bastions protruding from the main fort, each bastion having artillery, usually 24-pounder guns. The barracks, store, kitchen and magazine were housed in wooden buildings within the structure. There was a deep dry ditch surrounding the fort with a draw-bridge guarded by a wooden tower. It seems there was only one example built in Wales, and that was at Pill near Milford Haven (see pages 43-44). When the war ended in 1648, Parliament ordered the destruction of most of the castles in Wales so that they couldn't be used in a conflict in future. Several methods of destruction were tried, including blowing them up with gunpowder and undermining some of the walls and towers.

Pembroke Castle was much damaged in the second Civil War when it was besieged by Cromwell. After its surrender, the outer walls of the barbican and towers in the curtain wall were partially demolished, only being restored in the 1920s and '30s.

Eventually it was decided to make them uninhabitable by stripping them of all reusable materials.

By the 18th century the plan of a fort had evolved into a structure built of limestone reinforced with earthen banks. Forts of this kind were capable of containing a variety of gun calibres protected inside a casemate (a strongly built or armoured gun emplacement). The high towers of the castle age were replaced by buildings built into the wall structure. Some additional gun positions were built away from the main fort and protected by thick stone walls.

Throughout the 18th and 19th centuries France was Britain's usual enemy in Europe and the threat of invasion was often present. All the effort at defending the coastline was initially directed at the area bordering the English Channel. The west coast and Wales were regarded as safe from invasion as they were further away from the Continent, though a fort was built in 1750 on the edge of the dockyard at Paterchurch. This perception of security changed after the failed invasion at Fishguard in 1797, when it became clear that every coastal region was a potential landing place. Defence became a priority for national government, not just for isolated towns and wealthy individuals. Nevertheless, a government review of the defence of Britain in 1803 still only included the south coast and proposed to build a series of gun towers known as Martello towers. The original Martello towers were based on the design of a fortification at Cape Martella on Corsica. During the French Revolutionary War in 1794, this 16th-century fortification, held by a small garrison, had put up stiff resistance against two Royal Navy ships which bombarded the tower for two hours without causing any significant damage. Only after troops landed with field artillery did the occupants of the tower surrender Because of its design, the ships' cannon balls had largely glanced off the structure.

When the Duke of Wellington became prime minister, he pushed for a more effective coastal defence with its own designated troops in order to reduce the burden that was put on the Royal Navy and the army. His staunch ally was Lord Palmerston, who had often expressed the view that France was the nation's biggest threat. It was through his constant pressure that most of the next series of coastal forts were built. But it was not until 1849, following the Year of Revolutions on the Continent and with the succession of Napoleon III in France, that two gun towers were built to protect the royal dockyard at Paterchurch (Pembroke Dock). These two towers were completely different in design to the Martello tower and were built of brick with limestone and granite facing on three floors, with accommodation for one officer and thirty-three gunners, kitchen, stores, magazine and a 12,500 gallon water tank that was supplied by rainwater collected on the roof. They were armed with three 32-pounder Blomefield pattern smooth bore guns fitted on the roofs.

As the result of a Royal Commission in 1860, an additional twelve forts and fortified batteries were built at Milford Haven. Another fourteen were proposed but not constructed. Four additional forts and batteries were built on the Welsh side of the Bristol Channel, including two on the islands of Flat Holm and Steep Holm. This huge expenditure on fortifications placed a great strain on the treasury, just as it had when Edward I had proceeded with construction of his castles in the 1200s.

Often the building of the forts, though long planned, was the result of a hurried decision following events on the Continent. These massively expensive projects were also often obsolete before they were completed and within a short period were decommissioned to fall into neglect and ruin. It is doubtful whether those built in Wales were ever a deterrent against a French invasion and it is no wonder they became to be referred to as Palmerston's Follies.

However they came into their own during the two World Wars, especially in the Second when the gun positions were modified to take modern weapons, mostly for anti-aircraft purposes. Some fort walls and buildings were strengthened with reinforced concrete capable of withstanding high explosive bombs and shells, and others were fitted with quick-firing coastal artillery for the protection of shipping channels and ports.

3   The Threat of Invasion

In 854 AD the Viking chieftain Hubbu wintered his fleet of twenty-three ships in the Haven waterway and made several camps on the shore, one being at Hubberston, which was named after him. Whilst the Vikings threatened people along almost the entire coast (and navigable rivers) of the British Isles, thereafter until the 15th century any invasion threat was mostly focused on the south-east of England.

Even during the Civil War and subsequent wars with the Dutch there was very little development in fortifying the coast of Wales. Some lessons were learnt in England, however, when in June 1667 a Dutch fleet managed to pass the weak Medway defences, broke the boom across the Thames at Chatham and attacked installations and shipping. Soon an array of forts and other defences were built along the Thames to combat any future invasions. It was in Scotland, due to the Jacobite rebellions, and notably that which culminated in the battle of Culloden in 1745, that there was a resurgence in the building of fortifications, which included secure new roads linking the forts. The design of these new forts placed great importance on the ramparts and ditches, and included impressive earthwork defences. Entrance to each fort was across a glacis (an artificial slope of earth so constructed as to keep any potential assailant under the fire of the defenders), then a ditched ravelin (a triangular fortification extending out from the main walls), a bridge and a drawbridge, all protected by bastions with slits for muskets and cannons. These were essentially an improved Elizabethan design.

With the accession of William of Orange and Mary to the English throne, Britain became allies with the Dutch Protestant cause against France and her Catholic allies, resulting in two long wars, the War of the Grand Alliance (1689-97) and the War of the Spanish Succession (1702-

13). These wars made France the major threat to the British Isles, and because both France and Britain have long coastlines, the fear was raised that invasion might not just be focused on the south-east of England. The threat of invasion gave rise to several false alarms, and came close to becoming a reality in March 1689, when the French landed a small force and many supplies at Bantry Bay in Ireland, in support of James II. On this occasion the French fleet of twenty-four vessels was interrupted during unloading by nineteen English vessels which they drove off. Whilst no ships were lost on either side, the English suffered more than twice the casualties suffered by the French and their ships were so badly damaged that they were subsequently laid up in port for two months undergoing repair. The French failed to press home their advantage, however, and it was not until the War of the Austrian Succession of 1740 that they actually attempted to invade Britain, an attempt foiled by a severe storm in the English Channel.

Milford Haven in Pembrokeshire provided important sheltered water for the Royal Navy and other shipping, and in 1748 plans were put forward to build a small fort to protect the port of Paterchurch (Pembroke Dock) and the inner inlet. As far back as 1689 the Privy Council had been concerned about the protection of the Haven and especially Paterchurch, and instructed the Board of Ordnance to send an engineer to report on the type of fortification needed. Nothing was done until 1750, however, when, as already mentioned work on what became known as Pater Fort began in the north-western corner of the dockyard. It was constructed of timber and limestone with a stone-built barracks for its defenders within its walls. By 1759 the threat of invasion during the Seven Years War in Europe had passed and further construction work was suspended.

During the American War of Independence France supported the colonists in their war against Britain. In 1778 the American adventurer John Paul Jones, equipped with ships supplied by France, attacked and destroyed a shore battery at Whitehaven in Cumbria. This incident caused alarm bells to ring in Britain as it showed that any coastal area was vulnerable to enemy attacks from the sea.

Perhaps the most serious threat that arose during the American War of Independence was when a French general suggested that a force of

10,000 colonists could invade Britain while her army was fighting in the Americas. The plan was that they would land in Ireland with the help of a French fleet, and then proceed in smaller ships to the mainland. As Wales and especially Pembrokeshire faces Ireland, its coastline and ports could be the targets for invasion. The colonists rejected the idea, as it called for more troops than they had available. This was probably fortunate, for most of the defences around Milford Haven and the Severn Estuary had been built during the Tudor era and over the centuries they had been neglected. Stone walls and barracks were crumbling and unfit to house defenders, and most of the artillery pieces were of Civil War vintage, rusting and unsafe.

Whilst it was recognized by some that the Haven was of great importance as it provided a sheltered anchorage for naval and mercantile shipping, the government in London still felt that the priority area for rebuilding defences lay along the English Channel and in East Anglia. Nevertheless, an Act of Parliament in 1794 called upon 'gentlemen of weight or property' throughout the realm to initiate local defence plans that included the establishment of volunteer military formations. Three types were envisaged: infantry companies to man coastal artillery batteries, infantry companies to augment the regular militia, and cavalry. As a result of the Act, several Yeomanry Companies of Infantry were formed.

Just at the point when the British surrendered at Yorktown in America, the country was facing its next threat as the result of the French Revolution which began in 1793. Britain and France were more or less locked in conflict for the next twenty years, and the threat of an invasion was almost continuous, which necessitated immediate work on constructing new forts and protected batteries. In 1796 Spain joined France and declared war on Britain, adding considerably to the number of ships that could support an invasion, and on 15 December 1796 a fleet of forty-three ships carrying 15,000 troops, a large supply of arms and money, set sail from Brest. Once again their destination was Bantry Bay in Ireland. An easterly storm dispersed the fleet, and whilst some managed to reach Bantry Bay, others were blown round the coast of Ireland as far as Scotland, and on 27 January 1797 orders were given to abandon the expedition.

Perhaps the most remarkable invasion attempt took place on the Welsh shore later that year when a small French force under the command of the Irish-American Colonel William Tate and flying a Russian flag left Brest for England. Historians have debated the seriousness of the invasion, some suggesting it was a French scheme to test Britain's defence, others that its sole purpose was to cause panic in the population. The invasion force consisted of 600 regular troops and 800 convicts released from French prisons to fight for France, as well as three Irish officers. The force was lightly armed with muskets and cutlasses, and due to their black uniforms (which had been captured from the British in 1795 and dyed black) was referred to as La Légion Noire – the Black Legion.

The original plan was to land near Bristol, then England's second largest city, and the invaders were given orders to burn the port and cause as much panic as possible in the surrounding area. Because of storms and poor navigation, an alternative plan was formed to land troops in the Cardigan Bay area who would then march through Wales to Chester and Liverpool, hoping to persuade disillusioned inhabitants to join them. They were perhaps recalling Henry Tudor's famous march through Wales to Bosworth. As the four invasion ships, *La Résistance*, *La Constance*, *La Vengeance* and *Le Vautour* neared British waters they flew a British flag to confuse the local defences, but were sighted off Bishop Rock by Thomas Williams of Treleddyn, a master mariner, and recognised for what they were.

The French ships anchored off Carreg Wastad Point hoping to land at Fishguard, but after a warning (blank) shot had been fired by the coastal battery situated on the clifftop overlooking the harbour, being under the false impression that the town was heavily defended, they sailed on. This was fortunate for the coastal battery as they only had a store of blank shot, not having been issued with cannon balls. Colonel Tate then ordered his men to land at Carreg Wastad, a few miles from Fishguard. Within a short time seventeen boatloads of troops and supplies were landed on the shore, and under the command of one of the Irish officers, Lieutenant Barry St Ledger, the troops scaled the high cliff, carrying forty-seven barrels of gunpowder and twelve boxes of grenades, and established a base camp.

After pillaging some local farms and acquiring a stock of local brew, several of the French became drunk and were easily captured by the local people led by heroine Jemima Nicholas. Over the next few days the

*A view over the remains of Fishguard Fort,
and 9-pounder cannons still at the fort
(courtesy D. Evans, Pembrokeshire Coastal Photographs)*

rest of the invasion force were captured by the Pembroke Fencibles and the Cardiganshire Militia led by Lord Cawdor. On 9 March, the Royal Navy ships *HMS St Fiorenzo* and *HMS Nymph* pursued the invasion fleet, encountering first *La Résistance*, which had been crippled by bad weather in the Irish Sea, and then *La Constance*. After a brief skirmish both French ships surrendered. *La Résistance* was re-fitted and renamed *HMS Fisgard*, while *La Constance* was renamed *HMS Constance*.

The episode caused a certain amount of panic in Britain and increased awareness of the possible threat of an invasion. This threat was at its height between 1803 and 1805 when Napoleon Bonaparte's army was camped around Boulogne ready to invade the south coast of England on a fleet of barges built for the purpose. However, a series of ill-fated attempts to bring naval fleets to protect the barges culminated in the battle of Trafalgar in 1805, in which many French and Spanish ships were captured or destroyed. As a result, the invasion plan was dropped. Meanwhile, the construction of 88 Martello towers along the south coast of England had been authorised. Building began in 1805, although the threat of invasion had diminished, and by 1810 a total of 74 had been completed along the east and south coasts.

In Wales, meanwhile, several town and port batteries were upgraded and strengthened with emphasis placed on making sure they were properly maintained and armed, especially after the Fishguard fiasco. In Pembrokeshire two temporary batteries consisting of up to ten 32- and 18-pounder guns were sited south-east of St Katherine's church and at Hakin Point on either side of the town of Milford Haven between 1801 and 1803.

With the opening of the royal dockyard at Pembroke Dock in 1815 the defence of Milford Haven became a priority. In 1841 the fort known as the Defensible Barracks was built as both the landward defence of the dockyard at Paterchurch and to house the new garrison allocated to defend the dockyard. Its guns also had a clear view of the Haven.

Although Britain and France were allies in the Crimean War (1853-6), soon afterwards, when France was under the rule of Napolcon III, relations again deteriorated. Lord Palmerston, then Prime Minister for the second time and aged 75, had always had serious concerns about French intentions and in 1859 he set up a Royal Commission on the

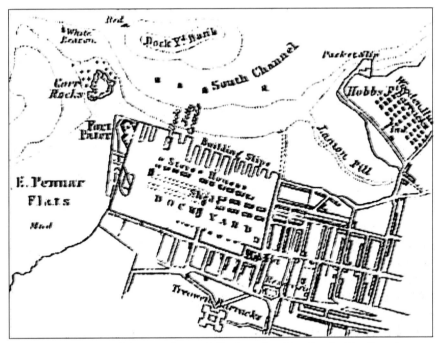

A plan of the royal naval dockyard at Pembroke Dock

Defence of the United Kingdom. Six eminent naval and military officers and a representative of the treasury were briefed to look into the state and competence of the fleet, fortifications, standing army and volunteer force, with a specific focus on naval dockyards. The Commission's report published in 1860 recommended the construction of new casemated forts in the royal dockyards at Portsmouth, Chatham, Plymouth, Portland and Milford Haven. In February 1860 the recommendation was placed before Parliament with an estimated cost of £12 million.

The forts were duly built, but within a short time they were classed as obsolete because of the rapid development in ship design. The armour of ships like the French *La Gloire*, a 5,630 ton wooden-hulled warship with 4 to 7 inch thick wrought iron side armour, armed with thirty-six 6.3-inch rifled muzzle-loaded guns, would easily have withstood the forts' guns. Over time the forts' armaments changed: smooth bore breech loaders gave way to rifled muzzle loaders (though these in turn were obsolete by

The French iron-clad warship La Gloire *which prompted the authorities to redesign and re-gun the forts in the Haven*

1890) and small calibre guns were replaced with guns of larger calibre. The standard 18-pounder cannon (the weight is that of the cannon ball) was replaced by heavier armaments. By 1900 the 68-pounder, one of the largest guns, lacked range and penetration and was deemed to be only effective against wooden-hulled ships. As a result, all fort and battery armaments were replaced by just four calibres of rifled breech-loaded guns: 9.2-inch, 6-inch, 4.7-inch and the 12-pounder quick-firing gun.

After France's defeat in the Franco-Prussian War of 1870-71, her status in Europe changed, but nevertheless, the British government remained wary of French aims in Europe. Yet events were to see Britain and France next as allies. As the result of the assassination of Archduke Franz Ferdinand of Austria the Austro-Hungarian Empire declared war on Serbia. As part of the Central Powers, Germany joined the war along-side Austria. France and Britain meanwhile had signed a defence pact with Serbia, and on 28 July 1914 the Great War (the First World War) began. Germany massed an army on the borders of the Low Countries and France, and eventually invaded.

For years the Germans had been planning how they would invade Britain should war break out, and several barges had been built and stored in secret. Yet it was from the air that the British people feared

Gun crew training on a 68-pounder gun c.1860
(courtesy Swansea Museum)

attack. After Zeppelins had bombed towns in England, rumours spread that they were to be used to carry troops for an invasion. Perhaps the British people's imaginations were far in front of the military planners.

The German army never invaded, but the country's submarines caused havoc around the coast of the British Isles including that of Wales. Several of the country's fortifications were re-gunned and manned, whilst an airship station and aircraft base was built at Milton and Fishguard Bay was equipped with seaplanes to combat the threat posed by the U-boats.

Perhaps the most serious threat of all came during the Second World War. The German Blitzkrieg had overrun much of Europe in a matter of months; the German army had invaded countries by land, sea and air. After the evacuation of the British army from Dunkirk, people readied themselves for an invasion, especially when the Germans, like the French before them, massed their troops in the ports along the French coastline, together with thousands of specially adapted barges. But like Napoleon, Hitler had first to secure and control the English Channel if he was to succeed.

German invasion barges in harbour in France in 1940

The Luftwaffe pounded British ports and airfields day and night hoping to destroy the RAF and naval shipping, but RAF Spitfires and Hurricane fighters during the Battle of Britain managed to deprive the Nazi war machine of air superiority. Just like Napoleon before him, Hitler had to give up his hopes of an invasion by sea. He cancelled his Operation Sealion and his army on the French coast was transferred to the eastern front for the invasion of Russia.

Although the immediate threat of invasion had passed, fortifications continued to be constructed, with the aim not just of coastal defence, but also of countering the threat of an invasion by parachutists. After the Battle of Britain, greater emphasis was placed on anti-aircraft batteries rather than coastal artillery. New gun emplacements were built to mount the standard 3-inch anti-aircraft guns along with the heavier 3.7-inch guns, supplemented by several mobile heavy and light units.

By 1944 and the landing of Allied troops in Normandy, the threat of a German invasion had been removed, and over the following years airfields were closed and gun emplacements were dismantled.

4   The Importance of Milford Haven

Milford Haven, being an ideal sheltered inlet for shipping, was a worth-while prize for any enemy; whoever controlled the narrow entrance to the inlet gained a stepping stone into Wales and beyond. Surprisingly, there is no record of any fortification controlling the waterway during the Roman occupation of Britain, although it is believed that Roman galleys must have sheltered in the Haven. The first recorded fortification in the area was built by the Normans on the site of Pembroke Castle in around 1093. A number of wooden watch towers were subsequently constructed along the shores of the Haven, and by the 12th century some of the towers had been replaced by stone structures built to deter the raids carried out largely by the Irish.

When Henry Tudor landed his troops in Milford Haven in 1485 and gained the throne of England he ushered in a period of relative peace. But his son, Henry VIII, whose reign began in 1509, took a keen interest in the defence of the nation. Before becoming king, Henry had travelled in Europe and studied current fortifications in various countries. In 1533 his divorce from Catherine of Aragon led to a breach with Rome, and the pope openly encouraged Catholic countries such as France and Spain to invade Britain.

In 1539 Henry commissioned Thomas Cromwell, his chief minister between 1532 and 1540, to make a detailed survey of coastal defences in England and Wales. As a result, Henry strengthened his navy and under-took an ambitious plan to build a series of 'Great Castles' – protected gun emplacements, blockhouses and forts – to protect his harbours and poten-tial landing sites. A total of twenty-four of these fortifications were built in great haste between 1539 and 1543 on the south coast, covering an area from Pendennis in Cornwall to Tilbury on the Thames. In Pembrokeshire recommendations were made to fortify Milford Haven with two bulwarks. However, it was another forty years before two blockhouses were eventually built on opposite sides of the Haven.

During the reign of Queen Elizabeth I, most of Henry's fortifications on the south coast of England were neglected and some even demolished, although Milford Haven's blockhouses had been re-gunned by the end of Elizabeth's reign. George Owen, a renowned local historian whose interest was historical buildings and structures, served twice as the Deputy Lieutenant of Pembrokeshire, from 1587 to 1590 and from 1595 to 1601. One of his responsibilities was the military defence and fortification of the Haven against a possible Spanish invasion. In 1595 he produced a detailed report based on a triangular formation of forts built on Thorn Island, Dale Point and Stack Rock, but the plan was shelved as the threat of invasion waned.

During the English Civil War Pembrokeshire largely supported the Royalist cause, with the exception of the town of Pembroke itself, whose castle held out as a Parliamentary stronghold in the area throughout the conflict. In 1643 the Royalists built a temporary fortification at Pill on the outskirts of the town of Milford Haven, but this was dismantled after the war (see Chapter 5).

In 1757 Lieutenant Colonel Bastide, the Director of Engineers, surveyed the waterway and recommended that six strong forts be built to protect the Haven at Dale Point, Bicton Point (Great Castle Head), West Angle, Popton Point, Paterchurch and Neyland, together with a floating battery on barges moored 500 yards north of Chapel Bay. The plan was dropped because of the cost and the limited range of the cannons at the time, a mere 500 yards. Ironically, the same sites were chosen later for fortifications.

The Admiralty was constantly in search of suitable sites for naval dockyards, preferably in sheltered locations and away from the Channel coastline, and the Haven had much to recommend it. The only drawbacks were its distance from the main centres of population (and so a workforce) and the awkwardness of reaching it by road (considering their state) or sea from the south-east of England. In due course the first naval dockyard on the Haven was constructed near the south-eastern shore of Hubberston Pill on land rented from Sir William Hamilton in

1800, but after a disagreement with the landlord the Admiralty moved its dockyard to a new site at Paterchurch (Pembroke Dock) in 1813. The royal dockyard was officially opened in 1815. The yard, built on an 80-acre site owned by the Meyrick family of Bush, was protected by high stone walls and gun towers. It grew in importance until by 1890 there were nearly 2,000 men employed at the dockyard constructing ships for the Royal Navy.

Some 260 battleships, cruisers, frigates, sloops, gun boats and five submarines were built between 1816 and 1922. Five royal yachts was also built at the dockyard, the last being *Victoria and Albert III* in 1859. The first two ships built at the yard were *HMS Valorous* and *HMS Ariadne*, two 28-gun frigates in 1816, and the last was *RFA Oleander*, an oil tanker built in 1922. Only seven of the ships built at Pembroke Dock were ever lost in action, whilst twelve were wrecked or lost in bad weather. The first Pembroke Dock built warship to be sunk during the First World War was *HMS Amphion,* followed by *HMS Warrior*, *HMS Defence*, *HMS Nottingham* and *HMS Drake*. The light cruiser *HMS Curacoa*, built in 1917, was lost with all hands during a collision with the liner *Queen Mary*. The yard closed in 1926 and the last vessels built at Pembroke Dock went to the breakers yard in 1956, these being the cruiser *HMS Andromeda* and the frigate *HMS Inconstant,* built in 1868.

In spite of the French landings in Ireland and then at Fishguard in 1797, no permanent defences were built during the French Revolutionary and Napoleonic Wars. Only temporary batteries were installed on either sides of the town of Milford Haven from 1801-03, at Hakin Point and south-east of St Katherine's Church.

In 1817, after a lengthy study, it was decided that fortifications should be built to protect the Haven and the dockyard from a seaborne land invasion. As usual nothing was done for a while, until in 1841 a defensible barracks overlooking the Royal Dockyard was built and manned by Royal Marines primarily to defend the dockyard from a landward attack.

During 1848, known as the Year of Revolution in Europe, further protection was planned for Milford Haven in the shape of two gun towers on either side of the dockyard. The north-east gun tower and the south-west gun tower, as well as the fort built on Stack Rocks, were each armed with three 12-pounder guns.

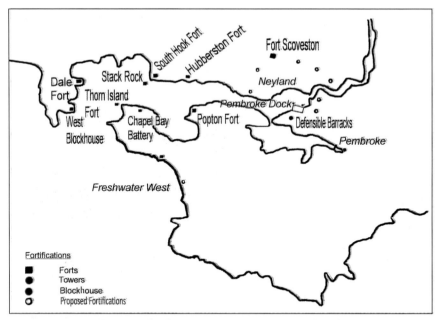

Map showing the location of the Victorian fortifications
of the Milford Haven waterway

Between 1850 and 1857, two forts were built at Thorn Island and at Dale, while on the site of the 1579 West Blockhouse a new fort was constructed.

Another governmental committee recommended that two lines of fortifications should be built to provide an ultimate defence of the Haven. As a result another phase of construction took place in 1859 with the building of forts at South Hook and Popton. Stack Rock fort was also strengthened with an enclosed and curved casemate battery.

The Royal Commission of 1860 recommended that the fortifying of Milford Haven be continued at all speed and at all cost, and so in 1861 work began on Fort Scoveston inland from the coast and on an elevated position with a clear view of the bay. Chapel Bay Battery was another fortification completed at the same time.

When the fortification programme was completed in July 1870 there were seven forts, one fortified battery emplacement, two gun towers and a defensible barracks protecting the dockyard and the inlet. The irony of

Protection of the royal dockyard at Pembroke Dock grew in importance the more ships it built for the Royal Navy. The 10-gun ironclad HMS Penelope *was built at the yard in 1867.*
(Courtesy National Maritime Museum)

The turret battleship HMS Dreadnought *built at Pembroke Dock in 1875*
(courtesy USN Historical Center)

these defences was that their armoury was already obsolete before they became operational, and with the introduction of the newer rifled guns, the forts had to be remodelled and modified to take the new artillery.

It is worth noting that there were proposed plans to build further similar forts at Pennar Farm, Bush Corner, Ferry Hill, Waterston, Honeyborough, Barnlake, Newton and Burton. Eventually the Treasury stepped in and prohibited any further spending as it was deemed that the nation could not afford it. The Royal Commission had also recommended that six forts should be built along the Pembrokeshire coast to protect the beaches and shoreline of Caldey Island, Lydstep, Freshwater East, Freshwater West and Tenby. However due to the total anticipated costs, only one was built, on St Catherine's Island in the shadow of Tenby Castle. Most of Milford Haven's defences were therefore built in one period and it has the largest concentration of coastal forts outside the English Channel area.

5   Fortifications in Pembrokeshire

All but two of the fortifications that were built between the reign of Henry VIII and the First World War in Pembrokeshire were to protect the waterway of Milford Haven. The other two fortifications were at Fishguard to protect the harbour, and at Tenby to defend against possible enemy landing sites. The following list in alphabetical order includes all these forts, gun batteries and other defences in Pembrokeshire.

Chapel Bay Battery

This is located some 2km from Angle and was built as the result of the Royal Commission of 1860.

The protection of the Royal Dockyard at Pembroke Dock was a high priority so the Commission proposed two new lines of defence to be built behind the West Blockhouse, Dale and Thorn Island forts to bolster the defences of the dockyard and port. One such fortification was the Chapel Bay Battery, or fort as it came to be known. Work began in the late 1880s and was completed in 1891.

The battery was the first fortification in the area to be built of mass concrete. It could accommodate 91 men in reasonable comfort with the usual mess room, sick bay and associated amenities. Initially the battery was armed with three 10-inch rifled muzzle-loading (RML) guns which were replaced by 7-inch and 9-inch breech-loading (BL) guns and eventually, in 1900, with three 6-inch breech-loading guns on central pivot mark II (CPII) mountings. Considerable changes were made to the design during the battery's construction when the French-constructed *La Gloire*, a wooden-hulled vessel with wrought iron side armour which made the fort's guns virtually obsolete (see pages 15-16).

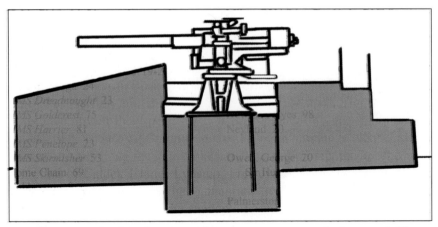

Drawing of a 6-inch gun emplacement on a central pivot mark II (CPII) mounting

Throughout the First World War the fort remained in military hands but it was decommissioned in 1920. The site has since been acquired by Mr George Geear who has restored the fort to its former glory and has opened it as a museum.

Dale Fort

This fort is located on Dale Point, giving it an all round view of the entrance to Milford Haven. The fort was built in 1850 to deter Napoleon III from invading the west coast of Britain and especially the sheltered inlet of Milford Haven. The fortification included a battery of cannons protected by an earth bank, and a few buildings constructed of stone. A new stone-built fort was built in 1856 as part of a triangular defence together with the West Blockhouse and Thorn Island fort.

Initially the fort was armed with one 80-pounder Millar pattern shell gun firing explosive shells, seven 68-pounder guns and two 32-pounder guns for landward defence. Accommodation was built for a garrison of 60 officers and men. When the fort was designed and built it was equipped with guns to counter wooden-hulled and sail-driven warships, but by 1871, with the introduction of iron vessels powered by steam, the fort and its armament were considered obsolete. In 1892 a new threat emerged in Europe with the formation of the Triple Alliance between

Chapel Bay Battery under restoration in 2008 (courtesy Mann Williams)

A restored 6-inch rifled muzzle-loaded gun at Chapel Bay Fort

Dale Fort from the air (courtesy Julian Cremona and Dale Fort)

The entrance to Dale Fort (courtesy Dale Fort)

Germany, Austro-Hungarian Empire and Italy, whilst France and Russia were in talks over an alliance. As a result the fort was reactivated which meant considerable alterations, including the installation of new armament such as the Zalinski pneumatic dynamite gun which could fire a 15-inch projectile of about 966lbs well over 4,500 yards. Up until this time it had been regarded as very dangerous to fire an explosive shell (in case it exploded within the barrel as that became hot), so Edmund Zalinski developed a gun which used compressed air to propel an explosive projectile. During a successful trial at Dale the paddle steamer *Harpy* was used as a target.

Within a few years a safer high explosive propellant called Lyddite was invented which proved to be more safe and efficient than previous such propellants, rendering the compressed air system unnecessary. Although the dynamite gun was dismantled, the garrison remained at the fort until 1902.

During the First World War, Dale Fort was used as a signal station for shipping in the vicinity, and was also part of the northern section of the Haven's boom defence against underwater attack.

Due to its prominent position at the entrance to Milford Haven, during the Second World War the fort was used as a Degaussing Range, its equipment measuring the magnetic signatures of ships to ensure they were not capable of setting off enemy magnetic mines. Electromagnetic coils were fitted in some ships to neutralize this signature, and a great number of degaussed ships were fitted out at Milford Docks.

When hostilities ceased in 1945 the fort was de-militarised and abandoned. Today it has been converted to a popular residential Field Studies Centre.

The Defensible Barracks at Pembroke Dock

The Defensible Barracks or, as it was known locally, Pembroke Dock Castle, is in many respects a fortress with gun emplacements, comprising a solid limestone wall with earthworks and a ditch or dry moat complete with a drawbridge. It is located on Barrack Hill, an elevated position within the town boundary. Work began on the fortress in 1840/41 and was completed in 1846 at a cost of £39,323 9s 9d. It is a good example of a Renaissance-style fortification, based as it is on a 16th-century Italian

*Two aerial views of the Defensible Barracks at Pembroke Dock
(showing the entrance on the bottom edge of the top photograph,
and to the right on the lower photograph), together with a plan of the
barracks opposite. (Photographs courtesy RCAHMW)*

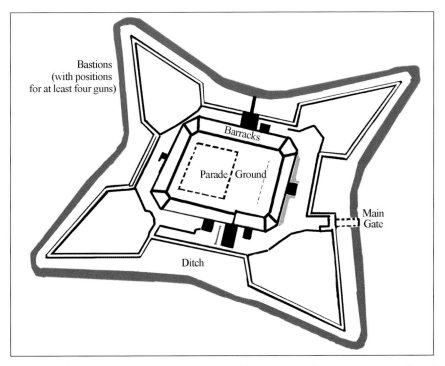

Bastions (with positions for at least four guns)

Barracks

Parade Ground

Main Gate

Ditch

design. The fort is diamond-shaped with gun emplacements at each of the four projecting corners. During its construction numerous properties in the area were demolished so to provide a clear line of fire for its guns. All the accommodation, mess halls, kitchens and basic hospital are located around a large parade square. From the outset it was designed to be a self-contained structure able to withstand any siege or attack. It had a system of collecting and filtering rainwater through a series of charcoal filters for storage in an 87,000 gallon underground watertank. From 1885 the fort was supplied by gas from the nearby Admiralty gas works. A normal garrison comprised 9 officers, 7 NCOs (Non Commissioned Officers) and 240 other ranks. The fortress armament included sixteen 24-pounder cannons (some of them upgraded later) with rifle loops for 663 muskets.

The main purpose of the fort was as a base for the Royal Marine personnel protecting the naval facilities at Pembroke Dock, especially the Royal Dockyard, from both seaborne and landward attack.

During both World Wars the barracks were manned by Royal Marines and used as a siege warfare training school. Arthur Lowe of Dads' Army fame was stationed there for a while.

Today the barracks have been given the status of a Grade II Listed Building and in 2010 they were put up for sale for £350,000. The cost of renovation has been estimated at in excess of £7 million.

Ditch and entrance to the Defensible Barracks

Part of the parade ground and actual barracks

East Blockhouse, Angle

As the result of a recommendation by Thomas Cromwell on behalf of Henry VIII, two fortified blockhouses – or bulwarks as they were referred to in manuscripts – were built on opposite sides of the entrance to the Haven: the East Blockhouse at Angle and the West Blockhouse at Dale. The East Blockhouse was built on a headland near to the location of an Iron Age Fort overlooking Castle Bay.

Both blockhouses were built in 1580 to a basic design comprising two-storey stone-built round towers with up to three cannon embrasures and positions for another three heavier calibre cannons on the strengthened roofs. There would also have been compacted ground nearby for positioning additional cannons. The design provided excellent all-round coverage of the entrance to the Haven and coastline nearby. Together with the blockhouse at Dale it would be nearly impossible for an enemy to enter the channel without coming under fire, albeit from mostly obsolete wrought-iron cannons.

Attached to the tower was a basic stone building usually for the officer in charge, a kitchen and sometimes a private toilet. The gunners' sleeping and messing arrangements were beside their guns, in line with the custom aboard naval warships.

In 1901 a Coastal Defence Battery emplacement was built in the vicinity of the East Block-house on East Blockhouse Point. It was completed in 1903 and comprised two gun emplacements for 9.2-inch guns with another three smaller emplacements for 6-inch guns added later. Brick-built buildings for the gun crews, officer quarters, cook house and latrines were built a short distance away.

During the First World War two 6-inch guns were withdrawn, followed by one of the 9.2-inch guns in 1917 as they were required on the Western Front. After a review of the Haven's defences, two 6-inch guns from the nearby

*The remains of Henry VIII's
East Blockhouse at Angle
(courtesy Peter Crane)*

Chapel Bay Battery were installed at East Blockhouse Battery in August 1918.

In 1937 the battery armament was modernised by the installation of two 9.2-inch breech-loading Mk X and two 6-inch breech-loading Mk VII guns. The two 6-inch guns were removed in June 1941 and installed at Lavernock Battery and replaced by a 12-pounder quick-firing gun. The guns were only used for training and practice firing and in 1944 the battery was disarmed, although ammunition did not leave the site until 1947.

The main Second World War artillery battery site was located to the south at Whetstone Hill just off the B4319 overlooking Gravel Bay, and consisted of four 3.7-inch MkII Anti-Aircraft emplacements. The guns could also be used to protect the nearby beach against an invasion. There is very little of the East Blockhouse remaining today; most of it has fallen into the sea as the result of cliff erosion. (The West Blockhouse was completely rebuilt in 1850 and still stands – see pages 56-8.)

Fishguard Bay Fort
Fishguard Fort is located on what today is known as Castle Hill, a natural defensive site on a headland overlooking Lower Fishguard and the bay, with a clear view of approaches to the town. It was built between 1779 and 1781 by the Lord Lieutenant Sir Hugh Owen at his own expense in response to the threat of privateers and smugglers in the area. The guns and the training of the local militia that manned the fort (also paid for by Sir Hugh) were provided by the Board of Ordnance. Powder and shot were reluctantly contributed by local businesses.

The fort was a simple construction with a 6 foot stone wall set across the headland surrounding the barrack block, store and magazine which also had a stone roof reinforced with earth. The entrance comprised a gateway with a solid wooden door. It was armed with eight 9-pounder smooth bore guns firing a cannon ball. Most of the cannons fired out through opened slits in the wall, although it is believed some were fitted on raised platforms.

The test came in 1797 with the arrival of the French invasion force. They initially intended to land in Fishguard but stood to when the fort fired a warning shot. Fearing that the town was well defended, the ships landed the invading force and its stores at Carreg Wasted Point. Afterwards, it

Fishguard Fort as it is today (courtesy David Evans)

The stone-built magazine at Fishguard Fort

emerged that the warning shot had been a blank round as the fort had not been issued with any cannon balls and the rest of the powder was damp. The French didn't know it, but the garrison consisted of just three Royal Artillery invalids and three lads from the local militia.

After the scare the garrison was increased and became the HQ of the Fishguard Fencibles. At the same time the magazine was restocked with new powder and shot, local businesses now being more eager to contribute, and a special emphasis was put on manning the fort. During the Napoleonic War it was proposed to build a larger fort in the area, but this never materialised. After the war the fort gradually fell into disrepair, its guns left to rust; it was soon only used as a look-out station manned by local militia.

During the Second World War, two .303 Lewis machine guns were installed with a concrete accommodation hut built further down the headland. Today the site is open to the public.

Hubberston Fort

Hubberston Fort is located on the west side of the inlet opposite Popton Fort and overlooking Gelliswick Bay. It was built as part of the chain of forts to defend Milford Haven. Work began on the fort in 1858 prior to the 1860 Royal Commission on the Defence of the United Kingdom and

Gun casemates at Hubberston Fort (courtesy David Evans)

was completed in 1863, but alterations and modifications continued until 1865.

The fort is of Victorian era design, being a D-shaped structure with a bomb-proof roof protecting the barracks and other buildings from such as mortar projectiles. It was protected on the landward side by a deep ditch and on the seaward side by a counter-scarp gallery (a gallery for muskets or light cannon built into the outer face of the ditch). The associated casemated battery is situated further down the headland and separated from the fort. Initially the fort and battery was to be armed with twenty-eight guns but only twelve were installed in the casemate, of which only eleven were protected by armoured shields. During an upgrade in 1870, eight guns on top of the casemate were removed and its roof was given a concrete plinth to support the Moncrieff gun pits (see drawing below) which replaced the earlier open pits.

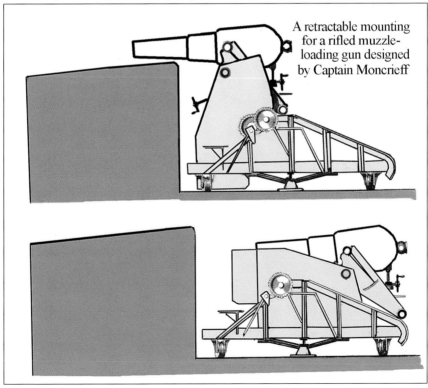

A retractable mounting for a rifled muzzle-loading gun designed by Captain Moncrieff

Drawing of a Moncrieff gun carriage

A Moncrieff gun carriage at Crownhill Fort, Plymouth, showing the typical layout (courtesy of Crownhill Fort)

Hubberston Fort's barracks (courtesy David Evans)

The fort was manned by 250 officers and men of the Royal Pembrokeshire Artillery and of the 24th Regiment of Foot. It became notorious in 1875, when a Lieutentant Walters was murdered by a Doctor Alder in a drunken brawl in the fort. According to orders from the War Office the fort was allowed to fire five live rounds a year for training purposes. However, in 1894 experiments were conducted at the fort when targets in the bay were illuminated by searchlights and the crews were permitted to fire additional rounds.

The battery was rearmed with 12-pounder quick-firing guns during the First World War but was abandoned in 1919. During the Second World War the fort was utilised as an air raid shelter by American army personnel stationed nearby. The Americans spent a considerable amount of money refurbishing parts of the fort, but it was never used.

After the war the fort fell into disrepair and became overgrown. Lately volunteers have spent considerable time clearing areas around the structure and inside. In 2009 local people filed a petition to save the fort, a campaign that still continues at the time of writing.

Pater Fort

Paterchurch, the old name for Pembroke Dock, had grown over the centuries to be an important port and town in the Haven. As far back as 1539 Thomas Cromwell had brought the town and port to the attention of the king and local dignitaries and as a result, two blockhouses were built to protect the entrance to the Haven, but not Paterchurch itself. In 1689 the town's Privy Council was also concerned about the vulnerability of the area. In 1748 the surveyor Lewis Morris, while surveying shipwrecks and navigation in the Haven, suggested that small forts should be built on Stack Rock and at Sandy Point and as a result plans were made for a small fort to be built on the north-western corner of the dockyard near what is known today as Carr Jetty.

Work on Pater Fort or Pater Battery began in 1750. The fort was constructed of timber and limestone blocks, complete with a self contained barracks. The outer wall was backed by earth for strength. By 1759 the threat of invasion during the Seven Years War had diminished and, like most projects in the area, further work was put on hold.

During an inspection of Milford Haven defences, the Inspector General of Fortifications, Robert Fenton, declared that the structure at Pater Fort was a 'scandalous waste of precious funds', and construction was completely halted.

As tension developed in Europe, the fort was reconditioned several times between 1830 and 1842 but was only garrisoned briefly in 1831. In 1842 a new battery (Paterchurch Battery) mounting twenty-three guns was built to protect the rapidly expanding royal dockyard. The battery was taken over by the Board of Ordnance in 1855 and renovated to designs by Lt Charles Gordon, who later was to lose his life at Khartoum. According to local records the fort was manned by dockyard volunteers and locally based units who often trained and drilled within its walls. In 1860 the volunteer unit changed its name to the Pembrokeshire Rifle Volunteers and within two years became the Pembroke Dock Volunteer Artillery. Practice firing was done against wooden barrels tied together and moored out in the bay, surmounted with a prominent flagpole. As the other defences in the Haven were built, the importance of Pater Fort diminished and in 1903 the battery and fort was dismantled; the stones were used to build structures in the town.

Pembroke Dock gun towers

Pembroke Dock has two gun towers built on either side of the dockyard, the north-east (Front Street) Gun Tower and the south-west (Fort Road) Gun Tower. The towers are of different design, the south-western one being angular in shape whilst the north-eastern tower is of an oval design. Both were built between 1848 and 1850 following what became known as the Year of Revolution on the Continent in 1848 and the resuscitated memory of the Fishguard landings of 1797. They were constructed of brick with limestone and granite facing. Although known locally as Martello towers they are in fact a completely different design to those built along the southern coast of England. Completion of the towers was delayed by building errors and unforeseen problems, and the guns were not installed until 1855.

The north-east tower was designed to accommodate one gun officer and thirty-three gunners manning three 32-pounder Blomefield pattern smooth bore guns on the strengthened roof of the tower. This gun had

The Front Street twin gun tower at Pembroke Dock
which now houses a museum

been designed by Major General Sir Thomas Blomefield, Inspector of Artillery at Woolwich Arsenal in 1780, and was the same design as that used by Nelson on *HMS Victory* during the battle of Trafalgar in 1805. Each gun was, however, attached to an iron carriage and traversing platform which allowed it to be turned through 360 degrees. Additional 12-pounder guns were mounted inside the tower with lines of fire to protect the dock wall flanks. By the late 1870s and the introduction of armoured warships and rifled guns firing explosive shells, the tower guns were regarded as obsolete. (The gun on present display in the gun tower is a smaller 18-pounder gun that came from Popton Fort.)

The tower contained separate officers' and other ranks quarters, together with a kitchen, two separate magazines, ablution rooms, a food store and a 12,500 gallon water tank which was supplied by rainwater collected on the roof. When gunpowder was being handled or delivered it was policy to cover the walls and floor with animal skin or thick felt to reduce a chance of a spark. All doors in the magazine were likewise covered in copper sheeting to reduce the likelihood of a spark, but barrels

An 18-pounder gun which came from Popton Fort now stands on the Front Street gun tower

of powder and shot had to be carried up narrow iron staircases to the guns on the roof.

The south-west tower was much smaller than that on the north-west, but was basically of a similar design. It could accommodate a garrison of twenty-four men and was armed with a 32-pounder Blomefield smooth bore cannon on the roof with two 12-pounder bronze cannons on each floor. It had a clear field of fire along the entire length of the southern dockyard wall as well as the approach to the dockyard from seaward and landward.

The south-west tower at Pembroke Dock

As the other forts in the area became operational the importance of the gun towers diminished. In 1881/82 the cannons were removed and the towers were not rearmed. However, during the Second World War twin .303-inch Lewis anti-aircraft machineguns was installed on the roofs and were actively involved during air raids in 1940 and 1941.

Today the north-east Gun Tower is a museum covering the town's military history, while the south-west tower is now privately owned.

Pill Fort

Most defensive structures built during the Civil War comprised earthen breastworks and gun platforms added as outer defences to various castles and fortified houses. Only one fort was constructed in Pembrokeshire. It was built by the Royalists in the autumn of 1643 on the west bank of Castle Pill (also known as Prix Pill), a raised headland at the junction of the Pill and the waterway, on the outskirts of Milford Haven. The Royalists' intention was to prevent the Parliamentarians from landing any troops to relieve Pembroke Castle and to make the area secure for the expected landing of Royalist supporters from Ireland. Because of its strategic importance King Charles authorised a sum of £400 to be paid towards the cost of building the fort and appointed Captain Steele to supervise its construction.

There is no definite description of the fort in county records but remnants elsewhere of these Civil War 'sconce' forts are very similar in design. They consisted of four earthen bastions with a ditch all around. The walls were of palisade (wood) and the cannons sat on the bastions with smaller calibre guns mounted on wooden platforms. The wooden magazine was covered with earth, whilst accommodation for the troops, kitchen and other stores would have been in wooden or tented constructions in the middle of the enclosure (see the drawing on p.5). The bell tower at nearby Steynton Church was used as an observation post and a musket tower.

Armament and ammunition for the garrison arrived by sea from Bristol in two Royalist ships, the *Globe* and the *Providence*. The fort was armed with eighteen cannons and a few mortars, and manned by nearly 300 troops.

On 23 February 1644 a Parliamentary force of three ships with troops and artillery under the command of Captain Swanley arrived in the Haven, Colonel Rowland Laugharne at Pembroke Castle assuming command of all Parliamentary land forces. In the meantime the *Globe* and the *Providence* took shelter in Prix Pill, protected by the guns from the fort. Parliamentary cannons were moved into position on high ground on the eastern side of the Pill and,together with cannons from the Parliamentary ships, bombardment of Pill Fort commenced on the morning of 24 February.

After the strongholds at Stackpole House and Trefloyne House fell to Parliamentary forces, Laugharne gathered together a force of 60 cavalry and 250 foot soldiers to assault the fort. Facing an overwhelming force on land and sea, the Royalist commander called a truce and surrendered. The fort was then manned by the Parliamentarians for the rest of the conflict. It was dismantled prior to the outbreak of the Second Civil War in 1648.

The earth embankments were still noticeable in the 1930s, but in 1990 the area was bulldozed and today bungalows have been built on the site.

Popton Fort
In 1757 Lt Colonel Bastide, Director of Engineers, recommended that a fort be built on Popton Point together with five other sites to protect Milford Haven, but it was a hundred years before anyone acted on that recommendation. The fort is located on the headland at the north-east corner of Angle Bay with a clear view of the bay, and opposite Hubberston Fort on the other side of the Haven. Both forts were part of the inner defence ring of Milford Haven.

Work commenced on the fort in 1859 and it was completed and fully armed in 1864 at a total cost of £76,700. It has tapering hexagonal ramparts with pentagonal bastions at the angles. It is surrounded by a large cleared area of sloping ground in front of the fort with just a ditch on the south side. Extending to the cliff edge on the west and north side are a two-tier casemate and an open battery facing west and north respectively.

There were eleven 9-inch 12 ton rifled muzzle-loaded (RML) guns in casemates, and one 10-inch and nine 9.2-inch guns in open emplacements. The barracks located at the rear could house ten officers, five staff sergeants and 158 other ranks with various facilities including canteen, wash rooms and a small hospital.

The west side battery was modified in 1869 to take six 7-inch guns on Moncrieff carriages (see p.38). There were no further upgrades or re-armaments and the guns were left to rust until they were dismantled in 1886.

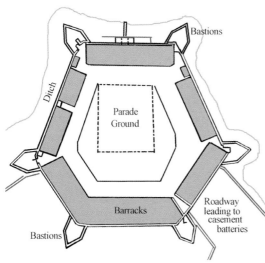

British Petroleum bought the fort in 1957 as part of its oil terminal, subsequently acquired by Texaco. The whole fort was altered and refurbished to accommodate the oil terminal facility.

Today it is a Grade II listed building and is preserved as one of Milford Haven's Palmerston's forts. Access to the site is only with permission of Texaco Ltd.

Aerial view of Popton Fort and its gun emplacements, and a plan of the fort (courtesy Texaco Ltd)

The west wall at Popton Fort with its gun casemates
(courtesy Landmark)

St Catherine's Fort, Tenby

The 1860 Royal Commission on the Defence of the United Kingdom recommended a ring of forts to be built along the southern coast of Pembrokeshire to protect the beaches of Caldey Island, Tenby, Lydstep, and Freshwater East and West, but only one was eventually constructed – that on St Catherine's Island (Ynys Catrin) at Tenby. The fort was designed by Lieutenant Colonel William Jervois, Deputy Director of Fortifications, and was built to defend the sandy beaches on either side of the island that could provide possible enemy landing sites.

The fort was built in the shadow of the remains of the town's 12th-century castle. Work began in June 1867 and was completed by 1876, but the guns were not installed until 1880 as the builders were waiting for special iron gun shields. Its design took full advantage of a 360 degree view of the surrounding area.

The fort had a series of gun casemates, the northern ones facing Tenby harbour, the beach and area towards Saundersfoot, whilst the southern casemates covered the coast towards Penally and Manorbier. Each casemate had three 7-inch rifled muzzle-loading (RML) guns behind a protected iron shield; there were two small caponier or rifle galleries to protect the entrance. On the roof there were three platforms for 9.2-inch RML guns, all facing the south-east. The fort accommodated several hundred soldiers in its barrack rooms. The magazines (which were capable of holding 444 barrels of gunpowder), a cartridge store and two main shell stores were all located in the basement at the east end of the fort.

St Catherine's Fort as seen from the land and the sea

St Catherine's Fort was fully garrisoned between 1873 and 1910, 1914 and 1918 and 1939 and 1945. During the Second World War it was manned at various times by detachments of troops from the Royal

St Catherine's Fort as seen from the air (courtesy Tenby Museum)

Marines, 4th Defence Battery Royal Artillery, elements from the Belgian Army, the Home Guard and the RAF ASR (Air Sea Rescue) unit who was responsible for the air sea rescue launch based in the harbour.

The fort was decommissioned by the military in 1959 and was sold for £10,000. For a brief period in the 1960s it was used as a zoo, and since then various plans and ideas have been proposed including a museum but none of them have come to fruition. However, there are plans to open the fort as a visitor attraction in 2013.

Scoveston Fort

The 1860 Royal Commission on the Defence of the United Kingdom proposed that a further six forts be constructed to protect the landward approaches to the Haven and the Royal Dockyard, but only one at Scoveston was actually built. Three contracts were issued in 1861, 1862 and 1864 to build various sections of the structure, and when it was completed in April 1864 it had cost £45,462, but even during its construction stage its role was in doubt.

Scoveston Fort is located inland in an elevated position with clear views of Milford Haven and Pembroke Dock across the Haven. It was of a hexagonal design surrounded by a rampart with a caponier on each corner. Outside, the land was cleared to form a glacis free of any obstruction for the fort's gunners. The rear face was defended by an earthen bank, and a large traverse was erected across the length of the interior parade ground. A 36-feet wide dry ditch surrounds the fort. Entrance to the fort is across a retractable drawbridge and a tunnel through a small gorge. The garrison could accommodate over 130 personnel in a bombproof barrack block.

Initially the fort was to be armed with an impressive 32-gun battery capable of hitting any invading ship in the Haven or deter a landward attack. However, the fort was not armed immediately because of cost but was recommended for arming during two military inspections in 1886 and 1898. In the 1900s forts began to lose their military importance and again due to the high cost it was decided not to install guns.

For the next few years the fort was maintained on a 'care and maintenance' basis. During the First World War it was used as the main training camp for the Milford Haven defences, with a complex system of trenches

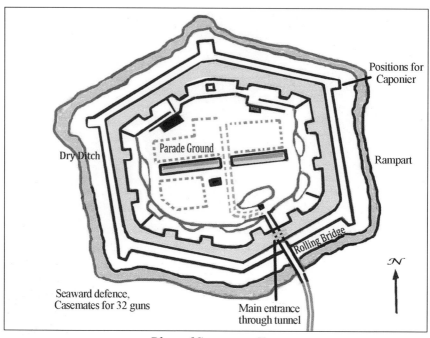

Plan of Scoveston Fort

Standard gun embrasures at Scoveston Fort

dug in surrounding fields that extended from Waterston via the fort to Port Lion, Llangwm. Throughout the 1920s and '30s the fort was abandoned but was kept in a reasonable condition. In the Second World War it housed several 40mm Bofor gun installations and its vast space became an ammunition store for the D-Day landings.

In 2004 the fort was classed as a listed structure. Today the fort is overgrown, although its structure is in good condition and is in the process of being preserved as a museum to be opened in the near future.

South Hook Fort

Work began on the fort at South Hook on 18 July 1859, a year before the report of the Royal Commission was published. The fort became part of the double defences of the Haven and was built to a similar design as that at Hubberston. It is D-shaped with walls 4 feet thick and contains a horseshoe-shaped two-storey barrack block. This is protected to the rear by a counterscarp gallery entered only by a tunnel from the barracks.

The fort comprised two separate batteries protected by earthworks and connected to the fort by covered walkways. The guns were mounted in embrasures with a magazine in between. Initially the fort was built to house a twenty-gun battery facing out to sea but it was modified during construction to take five 68-pounder smooth bore muzzle-loading guns and five 9-inch rifled muzzle-loading (RML) guns. Surrounding the fort was a deep ditch protected by three caponiers, and access to the fort was via a bridge.

The fort was completed on 31 December 1865, but was not fully manned until the following year.

In 1889/90 the western fifteen-gun battery was demolished to make way for two 10-inch breech-loading (BL) and three 10-inch RML guns, but because of cost only one 10-inch BL gun was installed. In 1886 the fort took part in a training exercise designed to teach soldiers how to defend a commercial port.

The fort's armament in 1895 was five 10-inch RML, seven 9-inch RML and two 6-pounder guns. In 1898 several D-plan gun emplacements were built for Maxim machineguns. This was again modified in 1904 when the fort became a coastal artillery battery unit armed with one 10-inch and three 6-inch RML guns, two 12-pounder quick-firing

An aerial photograph of South Hook showing the gun batteries along the clifftops and protective bank in front of the fort, together with the view of the fort as one approaches along the lane from the right in the top photo (courtesy RCAHMW)

guns and a number of Maxim machineguns. There was also a Defence Electric Light (DEL) searchlight unit manned by about 200 men. The fort's guns were aligned to provide crossfire with those at Hubberston and Popton Forts.

South Hook Fort was fully manned throughout the First World War although some of the guns were removed. The fort was abandoned in the 1930s and sold in 1936 but was requisitioned in 1939 by the Admiralty and called *HMS Skirmisher*. It was manned by WRENS controlling naval movements in the Haven while the Royal Marines provided protection with 40mm Bofor anti-aircraft guns. After the war the base was decommissioned and returned to private ownership. Today it is part of the liquid natural gas terminal jetty.

Stack Rock Fort

Thomas Cromwell in his report in 1539 drew the king's attention to the lack of defence protecting the entrance to Milford Haven. He proposed a fortified blockhouse on Stack Rock to protect the entrance to the inlet; however, two were eventually built on other sites.

Stack Rock came to attention again in 1748 when Lewis Morris, who was carrying out a survey of shipwrecks and navigation in the Haven, recommended that a small fort be built here. The subject was brought up again in 1817 by Colonel Bryce and once more by Colonel Burgoyne in 1850. By then the defence of the royal dockyard at Pembroke Dock and the sheltered inlet of Milford Haven had come to be seen as paramount in any future conflict. Work on construction was commenced in 1850 and completed in 1852.

The fort was originally designed for two decks of artillery casemates carrying a total of 45 guns, but only the ground floor was fully completed and used as a gun deck, while the first floor accommodated a garrison of one officer and thirty men. (The fort was designed with the capacity for a garrison of 250 men, although as it transpired the garrison never exceeded 150 personnel at any one time.) The basement was used for storage of food and water and the fort's magazine. The roof originally had an earth covering but this was removed during subsequent redevelopment and upgrading. In 1855 the fort was armed with just three 32-pounder guns and one 12-pounder. In 1859 new guns were installed,

Stack Rock Fort (courtesy David Evans)

including sixteen 10-inch and seven 9-inch rifled muzzle-loaded (RML) guns. In 1895 the armament was reduced to five 10-inch and seven 9-inch RML guns, but with an additional two 6-pounder guns. Four 12-pounder quick-firing (QF) guns were added later. At one point it was proposed to install two 25-ton guns on the roof but the plan never materialised.

During the First World War only two 12-pounder QF guns and a searchlight remained at the fort, which was only manned by a small contingent. In 1929 all armaments were removed from the fort including several 10-inch shells dating to the 1871 era. The fort was sold in 1932 for £160, and in 2005 it was up for sale again – but this time the price tag was £150,000.

Thorn Island Fort
Thorn Island Fort was one of the last to be built specifically to combat wooden sailing ships. Constructed on a two-acre rocky islet about a quarter of a mile offshore near the entrance to Milford Haven in 1854, it was one of the three forts of the outer Haven's defence ring protecting the entrance and the Royal Dockyard in Pembroke Dock.

The fort was built of limestone and concrete, to a design similar to that of other forts in the area. It is positioned on the highest ground to the west behind a low parapet. To the rear of the battery is the parade ground, surrounded on three sides by a vaulted single-storey barracks and associated buildings. The northern section consisted of a cook house and officers' quarters. The eastern section consisted of the other ranks barracks and the main entrance to the fort, with a strong guardroom occupying a small bastion in the centre. Another officers' quarters was situated in the south range. At the western edge of the southern range was the armoury and magazine protected by a stone-built half-round bastion protruding from the exterior wall. The barrack block had a flat roof with access to both the east- and south-facing parapets with holes for small arms fire. A bridge connected the narrow gap between the south and east range. Underneath the small parade ground there were three reservoirs capable of holding 30,000 gallons of water. To the rear there was a walled enclosure with gun emplacements.

The fort was armed with a barbette (raised gun platform) battery of nine 68-pounder smooth bore muzzle-loading guns and was manned by a garrison of over 110 men.

An aerial view of Thorn Island Fort (courtesy Christies)

With the introduction of steam and iron ships the fort and its armament were obsolete by the end of the 19th century. The 68-pounder guns lacked range and penetration and were only effective against wooden-hulled ships. In 1901 its armament was upgraded to take 5-inch breech-loading (BL) guns and 3-inch quick-firing (QF) guns.

During the First World War a Defence Electric Light (DEL) (a searchlight) was installed at the fort, overlooking the boom defence which ran between the fort and Dale Point.

In 1932 the island was sold and the fort became a hotel; however it was requisitioned in 1939 and used by the Admiralty. In 1947 it was returned to private ownership and resumed life as a hotel.

Since then it has been totally refurbished, but in 2011 the company owning the hotel went into administration and the hotel is up for sale for £750,000.

West Blockhouse

In 1539 Henry VIII commissioned Thomas Cromwell to make a detailed study of the defences of his kingdom. As a result Henry built up his

The walls of the West Blockhouse date to 1850

Gun emplacement with central pivot at the West Blockhouse, and a 9.2-inch coastal gun at the blockhouse during the First World War

navy to be one of the most powerful in Europe, but he was concerned about coastal protection of his realm. He therefore began an ambitious defence scheme by building a chain of forts, gun batteries and gun towers to protect harbours and potential landing sites. Although at the time Cromwell drew attention to the need to fortify Milford Haven, another forty years passed before any fortifications appeared. In 1580 two blockhouses, or bulwarks as they were referred to, were built to guard the entrance to the Haven, one being the West Blockhouse on West Point located between Mill Bay and Watwick Bay.

The present blockhouse was built on the same site in 1850, and at the same time as the fort at Dale across the entrance of the Haven. Construction was of limestone and granite. It was armed with the standard weapons of the period, six 68-pounder smooth bore guns, and was manned by a garrison of thirty-four men and one officer. In 1901 the fort's gun emplacements were remodelled to take four 5-inch breech-loading (BL) guns mounted on Vavasseur carriages (a recoil gun mounting invented by Josiah Vavasseur) and two 3-inch quick-firing (QF) guns on the roof of the blockhouse.

In 1904/05 further gun emplacements were built on the clifftop above the old fort, which included two 9.2-inch breech-loading Mk X guns and three 6-inch Mark VII coastal guns. This armament remained throughout the First World War, garrisoned by men of the Royal Artillery. During the Second World War it was classed as an Examination Battery, checking shipping entering and leaving Milford Haven. Supplies to the fort were landed nearby at Watwick Bay.

After the war the blockhouse was decommissioned. In recent years the fortification has been restored by the Landmark Trust to provide holiday accommodation.

6   Pembrokeshire in two World Wars

As air power developed it was inevitable that Pembrokeshire would be chosen as the location for military training establishments further from the reach of Continental-based air power. Some of these would be airfields, some of which would accommodate long range aircraft able to provide some protection for convoys from U-boat attack.

At the start of the First World War, it was however as a base for mustering infantry that Pembrokeshire first saw 'active service'. In August 1914 local yeomanry were mustered and put on standby, while coastal and Victorian forts were reactivated and manned. Before the end of the year tented army camps emerged in almost every part of the county.

In the early part of the war the greatest threat to the British coast and shipping was posed by the warships of the German High Seas Fleet. It began its shipping attacks in the traditional way by using its surface raiders, mostly cruisers, where the Allied naval forces were at their weakest. Within months many of the German cruisers and raiders were hunted down by the Royal Navy and sunk, and others were blockaded in their home ports with the rest of the German High Sea Fleet.

A new threat in the shape of U-boats then emerged to threaten shipping. These were capable of slipping out of German bases undetected and harassing ships well away from their bases.

The First World War U-boat campaign began on 4 February 1915, when the German High Command announced that ships in the vicinity of Britain and Ireland were legitimate targets. Initially there was a gentlemanly agreement under which civilians were put in lifeboats before the ship was sunk, but soon the style of warfare developed into torpedoing cargo ships without warning.

The shipping lanes around the Welsh coast were of the utmost importance to the war effort, providing a route for importing essential food and raw material for industry. In addition various parts of the country relied on coastal freighters to ship coal from many of the country's coal fields. Welsh coal was the main power source for the Royal Navy ships based around the UK before conversion to oil, and this too was shipped by coastal freighter.

The Bristol Channel and the Western approaches were therefore a high risk area as they were on the sea routes to the south Wales and West Country ports, and via the Irish Sea and St George's Channel to the ports of Belfast, Holyhead, Liverpool and the industrial areas of Merseyside. To counter U-boat attacks and provide limited protection to shipping, a convoy system was activated, with naval escort and air patrols. Even so, in 18 months 1,300 merchant ships were sunk in the Atlantic and in home waters. Three-quarters of the merchant shipping lost in 1917-18 were sunk within 50 miles of the coasts of Britain and France, with four out of every ten sunk 10 miles off the coast, usually in sight of land.

In the early years of the war the aeroplane was in its infancy and was only used for observation, the War Ministry and the Admiralty believing that only warships were capable of protecting the sea lanes from German surface raiders and U-boats. But as better planes were designed with more powerful engines, aircraft speed and endurance increased and planes were able to carry more and better armaments. By 1918 the aircraft had developed into a formidable weapon, especially with the introduction of the twin-engined bomber.

As the Admiralty view of the capacity and use of the aeroplane changed, Pembrokeshire was seen as an ideal location for both seaplane and airship bases. Two Royal Naval Air Stations were therefore established, a seaplane base near the northern breakwater of the port of Goodwick at Fishguard Bay, and an airship station at Milton known as RNAS Pembroke. The former had a single slipway for the seaplanes and launching crane on the breakwater, with three adjoining wooden buildings and a Bessonneau hangar which housed the seaplanes. Further buildings were added later to house accommodation, a wireless room, guard room, women's rest room, photographic hut and workshops. The officers were billeted in the nearby Fishguard Bay Hotel. The base was officially classed as operational in March 1917 by Squadron Commander John T. Cull, DSO, RN of the Admiralty Air Department Special Service, but the first seaplanes were not delivered until 13 April 1917. The station's patrol area was the northern coast of Pembrokeshire, especially the Irish Sea route between Fishguard and Cork, and an area covering from Cardigan Bay to St Govan's Head in the south of the county.

There were two naval seaplane flights stationed at Fishguard equipped with Sopwith Baby and Short Type 184 aircraft. The Sopwith Baby, built by Blackburn Aircraft and Fairey Hamble, was the smallest of the seaplanes. It was a single seater and was powered by an 110hp Clerget engine which gave it a speed of 92mph and two hours flying time (or endurance) in fair weather. It was armed with a single .303 Lewis machine gun and could carry up to 130lbs of bombs. The two-seat Short 184 was much larger and was powered by a 200-240hp Sunbeam Mohawk or Maori, or a Renault engine, which gave it a speed of 88mph and an endurance of five hours. Its armament was a .303 Lewis machine gun in the rear cockpit and either a 14-inch torpedo or up to 260lbs of bombs. The two flights became No. 245 squadron on 20 August 1918, standardizing on one type, the Short 184.

The 1918 seaplane base at Fishguard
with maintenance sheds and hangar

The area occupied by the crane in this photograph of Fishguard harbour was the site of the First World War hangar and maintenance sheds

The squadron was disbanded on 10 May 1919, by which time it had been reduced to a few aircraft, and by the end of the month the station was closed. There are no records of any submarine being either damaged or sunk by Fishguard-based seaplanes, although several sightings were reported. However, their presence was a deterrent, as on a number of occasions surfaced submarines made a hasty retreat when a seaplane was in the vicinity. Most of the base infrastructure was dismantled and removed in 1919. Today the slipway still remains and the dock area is used by private vessels and the Fishguard lifeboat.

The other First World War station was that for airships at RNAS Pembroke. This occupied some 228 acres near the village of Sageston, just off the main road between Pembroke and Carmarthen. The station consisted of a 112 feet x 338 feet corrugated iron hangar with associated windshields and other infrastructures. Accommodation consisted of a mixture of wooden and canvas huts just off the main road. The station was officially opened in August 1915 and was classed as fully operational in April 1916. For some years the Admiralty had been using dirigibles for fleet reconnaissance operated from ships and land bases. Their long endurance made them ideal craft for patrols and convoy escort. RNAS

Sea Scout Zero airship (SSZ 17) taking off from RNAS Pembroke
(courtesy Fleet Air Arm Museum)

Pembroke operated a range of airships, including the Sea Scout SS type, the large Coastal class and the Sea Scout Zero SSZ type, which were actively involved in patrolling the sea lanes and the Western Approaches. Fully loaded, the Coastal type could carry half a ton of bombs, was armed with two .303 Lewis machine guns and had an endurance of twenty hours. There are no records of any of Milton's airships sinking any submarines, although several were involved in sighting them and directing surface ships to the scene. Again, the airships' presence during escort duties and patrolling was a deterrent. After Armistice Day the airships were involved with Royal Navy minesweepers in clearing the coastline of mines.

In 1917 the Admiralty realized that since the introduction of the convoy system and airship patrols, the majority of merchant shipping losses had been within ten miles of land. These attacks were well within the then limited range of aircraft combat radius. In April 1917, therefore, three Bessonneau hangars were built in the south-east corner of the airship station for Nos 519/520 Flights of No. 255 squadron equipped with Sopwith 1½ Strutter bombers, later joined by Airco DH 4 aircraft. Initially seven aircraft were destined for Pembroke, but one was damaged en-route.

The Sopwith 1½ Strutter was a single-seat fighter-bomber powered by an 110hp Clerget engine which gave it a speed of 108mph. The aircraft was armed with one forward firing Vickers machine gun and a .303 Lewis machine gun, and could carry four 25lb bombs. The Strutter aircraft got its name from the unusual arrangements of short and long pairs of centre section struts. The Strutters patrolled an area between the shoreline and up to 100 miles off shore, covering the coast from Milford Haven to the Gower Peninsula.

All the Coastal Patrol Squadrons, including No. 255 at RNAS Pembroke, were disbanded on 14 January 1919. In 1920 the Admiralty relinquished the site and the buildings were eventually demolished. All traces of the airship station vanished during the building of an airfield on the site some ten years later.

It was not only airfields that were built for defence in Pembrokeshire during the First World War. The Royal Navy was considered to be the main defence in the event of an invasion, and warships were stationed in several locations around the British Isles. It became apparent, as the war progressed and warships were needed in other theatres of war, that the Royal Navy could not sustain a constant vigilant watch on all the British coastline. The reintroduction of coastal batteries therefore became paramount to the nation's defence, with existing batteries being repaired and new ones constructed.

Of the batteries repaired in Pembrokeshire, some were modified to take up to date guns, while others became barracks and some were used for training. In Pembroke Dock the Defensible Barracks, manned mostly by Royal Marines, was used as a siege warfare training school. Other forts were used to house troops manning the anti-invasion defences in the area, with Scoveston Fort being the main camp. The two batteries at the mouth of the Haven were manned and kept operational until the end of the war.

At Thorn Island Fort a defence electric light (DEL) was built overlooking the boom which was installed between the fort and Dale Point.

The Second World War

In 1940, after the fall of France and the retreat from Dunkirk, it was felt that it was only a matter of time before the Germans would invade Britain. The government planned to try and hold any invasion on the coast, with mobile reserves able to be brought quickly into play. To counter the threat of diversionary airborne attacks and acts of sabotage, the Home Guard was instigated so as to leave regular troops free to counter the main invasion thrust. To deal with the contingency that invaders might not be stopped on the coast but might manage to get further inland, a number of stop lines were constructed, using natural barriers such as rivers and canals, to try to halt any enemy advance. In Wales nine stop lines were constructed as part of the Western Counties stop line system, which consisted of pill boxes, concrete block obstacles, barbed wire, old railway lines and ditches. Twenty-seven Welsh beaches were also protected with various obstacles and mines, including those in Pembrokeshire.

A 6-inch quick-firing Naval Gun which became a common coastal armament during the Second World War, replacing the early 1900s models (courtesy Vickers)

In Pembrokeshire the Home Guard patrolled the cliff tops and every inlet, looking out for signs of any enemy activity. Meanwhile the Royal Observer Corps, formed in 1939, established observation posts located usually 10 miles apart to record and pass on information about enemy aircraft movements. These provided valuable information to the anti-aircraft batteries located in the county.

Just as during the First Word War, several of the 19th-century fortifications were re-activated by the military, especially those in prominent coastal locations. The two-gun emplacement at East Blockhouse Point at the entrance to Milford Haven was manned throughout the war by men of the Royal Artillery. As well as guarding the entrance, their second role was as an 'Examination Battery' responsible for checking all sea traffic leaving and entering the port. Pembroke Dock's two gun towers were used to house anti-aircraft Lewis machine guns. Several anti-aircraft gun batteries were also built at Bateson, Bateman Hill, Rosemarket, Steyton, St Daniel's Hill, St Ishmael (Great Castle Hill, a light anti-aircraft battery and searchlight) and Whetstone Hill near Angle in the Milford Haven

An aerial view of a heavy anti-aircraft gun battery installation at Whetstone Hill, Freshwater West in Pembrokeshire. Note the resemblance to the Victorian layout (courtesy APC)

The heavy anti-aircraft gun emplacement at Whetstone Hill
(courtesy APC)

area. The Whetstone Hill battery was located just off the B4319 over-looking Gravel Bay and consisted of four 3.7-inch MkII anti-aircraft emplacements. The guns were controlled from a concrete rectangular command post equipped with a mechanical predictor which could calculate the height and speed of an approaching enemy bomber. The guns could also be used to protect the nearby beach in the event of an enemy landing.

Pembrokeshire had numerous gun emplacements. This 9.2-inch coastal
gun with a Sunderland flying boat in the distance is at Angle
(courtesy Imperial War Museum)

Most of the other anti-aircraft batteries were mobile. These batteries were accompanied by searchlight units, either in the open or in a purposely built concrete bunker. Most of the anti-aircraft batteries were installed after the 1940/41 bombing raids on Pembroke Dock and other parts of the county. The most common calibre gun used by the anti-aircraft batteries in the county was the First World War vintage 3-inch quick-firing (QF) gun until it was replaced by the 3.7-inch gun.

A coastal battery was built at Fishguard at Penrhyn Ychen (near Dinas Cross), which housed two 6-inch QF guns and 3 inch unrotated projectiles (UP) rocket launchers. Other fortifications were utilised in various ways as air raid shelters, for training, as look out posts by the Home Guard and as secret bases for covert operations.

As the war progressed, a string of radar installations were built around

Aerials at RAF Hayscastle Cross in 1944 (courtesy Subbrit)

Entrance to the underground operation room at RAF Hayscastle Cross (courtesy Subbrit)

Radar was developed during the Second World War and several radar stations were built in Pembrokeshire. In 1941 the original temporary wooden huts were replaced by concrete bunkers like the one here at St Twynnells.

Inside St Twynnells in 2009 (courtesy Nick Catford)

Wales for the detection of shipping and aircraft, and various masts and aerials appeared on the skyline. The main radar stations in Pembrokeshire were at Folly, Hayscastle Cross, Kete, Warren and St Twynnells, all built between 1940 and 1942, and formed part of what was called Home Chain, a ring of coastal early warning radar stations. The initial temporary wooden buildings were eventually replaced by brick-built structures. In the 1950s they became ROTOR sites and were situated in semi-sunken bunkers. ROTOR was the codename for an elaborate radar system built in the 1950s to counter possible attack by Soviet bombers; it incorporated many of the Second World War Home Chain sites. RAF Kete, a radar station built to track low-flying aircraft, was located a short distance south of the site of Dale airfield. When the Admiralty took over the airfield, Kete became a Royal Navy Fighter Direction School and a Naval School of Meteorology. It remained so until the station closed in 1960.

Look-out stations also became common around the coast, while searchlight batteries and barrage balloon units were located near to towns and military bases.

The remnants of the war can be seen all around the county, whether they are the various concrete or brick pillboxes, the concrete tank obstructions, or the watch towers, radar installations, searchlight blockhouses and gun emplacements found in prominent locations around the coast. Other relics of war found in the county vary from the numerous army

A 3.7-inch anti-aircraft gun being fired at the Army School of Artillery at Manorbier

An inspection of a 3.7-inch gun heavy anti-aircraft battery

A Second World War 6-inch gun emplacement overlooking Fishguard Bay

The main light anti-aircraft gun during the Second World War was the 40mm Bofors gun.

Throughout the county there are still a number of Second World War pillboxes. This one is located on the outskirts of Haverfordwest.

The stump of a 17th-century windmill at Angle was utilised to create a pillbox for the nearby airfield.

Right: One of the entrances to the underground storage tunnels at RNAD Trecwn. The depot made and stored shells for the Royal Navy during the Second World War (courtesy Ruston Register).

Derelict buildings at the Royal Naval Armament Depot at Milford Haven

camp barracks such as Llanion and Pennar Barracks, the Royal Naval Mine Depot at Milford, the tank training ground at Castlemartin, and the Royal Naval Armament Depot at Trecwn.

Of all the Second World War installations, perhaps it is the airfields that have most obviously left their mark on the landscape, and these are covered in the next chapter.

7 Airfields in Pembrokeshire

When war was declared on 3 September 1939 there were only two permanent RAF stations in Pembrokeshire: a flying boat station at Pembroke Dock which was opened on 1 January 1930, and the support airfield at Carew Cheriton, opened in 1939. There was also a temporary grass landing ground at the Artillery School at Manorbier. During the early war years there was a great urgency to build new airfields in Pembrokeshire as the peninsula was ideally suited for Coastal Command operations in the Atlantic and the Bay of Biscay. By 1945, ten military airfields had been built, including operational airfields, a seaplane station, satellite airfields, and relief landing grounds, with a mixture of concrete runways and grass landing areas.

Angle

RAF Angle was planned and built during 1940 and was declared operational in May 1941. The airfield was located just off the B4320 which connects the village of Angle with Pembroke. On 1 December 1941 RAF Angle became a forward base in the Fairwood Common sector under No. 10 Group, Fighter Command whose responsibility was to provide fighter cover for south Wales and the south-west of England. The airfield had three surfaced runways, the longest being 4,800 feet long. There was one T2 hangar, four Over-Blister-type hangars and fourteen dispersal pens were located on the south-eastern side, each large enough for four single-engine fighters.

The first squadron to use the airfield was No. 32 squadron with its Hawker Hurricanes in early June 1941. Between 1941 and July 1943 several fighter squadrons operated from the airfield on convoy patrols and air defence of south Wales, including No. 263 squadron, which operated Westland Whirlwinds and No. 421 squadron, Royal Canadian Air Force, which flew Spitfires. In July 1943 the airfield was temporarily taken over by the Fleet Air Arm, but in September it was transferred back to the RAF for training purposes.

On 29 May 1943 a Short Sunderland piloted by F/O Gordon Singleton made the first ever dry landing by a flying boat on an airfield, the aircraft having been damaged during take off in heavy weather.

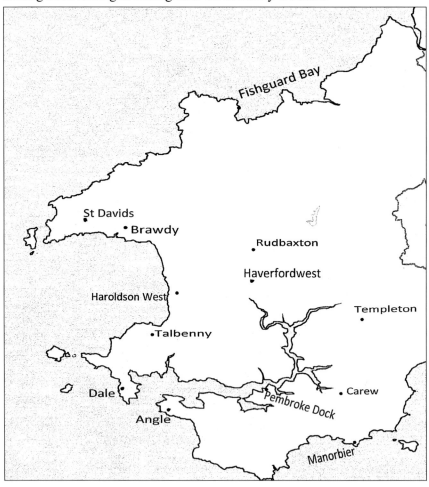

Map showing the location of airfields and seaplane bases in Pembrokeshire

RAF Angle was officially closed on 1 January 1946 and the land has since been returned to agricultural use. All the runways, perimeter track and dispersal pens have been ploughed up. The firing butts were until recently the only wartime structures left. However, the layout of the airfield can still be clearly seen from the air.

Brawdy

Brawdy Airfield is situated just off the A478 between Haverfordwest and St Davids. The airfield became operational on 2 February 1944 as a satellite to nearby St Davids, under the control of RAF Coastal Command. However, on 1 November 1945, the station headquarters and its squadrons were officially transferred from St Davids to Brawdy, reversing the hierarchy and leaving the former to become a satellite airfield.

Brawdy had three runways, two of which were 6,000 feet in length and capable of operating the heaviest Coastal Command aircraft of the time. There were 27 spectacle-shaped dispersal points around the airfield. The main technical and administration site was on the west side situated between two of the runways, while the main accommodation site was situated between the airfield and the main road. Only one T2 hangar was built during the Second World War for maintenance and storage, another two being added when the headquarters moved from St Davids in 1945.

The main squadron based at Brawdy was No. 517 Meteorological squadron, equipped with Handley Page Halifax aircraft, although other Halifax squadrons (Nos 58 and 502) also used the airfield. In January 1946 the airfield was handed over to Admiralty control.

It was not until 1951 that extensive modernization took place. The runways were lengthened by 500 feet and all taxiways and dispersal points resurfaced. Several new Mainhill and Main hangars were built. The control tower was modified to a standard Admiralty three-storey design. The revamped airfield (renamed *HMS Goldcrest*) was declared operational in 1956.

The Fleet Air Arm used Brawdy for training and it also provided a shore base for Royal Navy aircraft carriers while in port. The most common aircraft types seen at the airfield were Sea Hawks and the resident Fairey Gannet anti-submarine aircraft.

A line-up of the Fleet Air Arm's Fairey Gannet aircraft at Brawdy

With a number of Royal Navy carriers being decommissioned, Brawdy was declared surplus to requirement and the RAF took control of the airfield again in 1971. Only minor alterations were done to the infrastructure.

Under the name of RAF Brawdy the airfield became the base for the Tactical Weapons Unit (TWU) initially equipped with Hunters and then the Hawk trainer. The TWU was disbanded in August 1992 and soon afterwards the RAF moved out.

Aerial photograph of Brawdy Airfield in 2009

However, in 1996 part of the base was taken over by 14 Signals Regiment, Royal Corp of Signals, after extensive alterations, and became known as Cawdor Barracks. As the Signals Regiment only use part of the site, by 2013 half the airfield infrastructures including the control tower and some of the hangars had been demolished. The runways are sometimes used for civilian motor racing.

Carew Cheriton

Carew Airfield was located more or less on the site of the First World War airship station. Construction took place during the summer of 1938 and it was opened a year later. Carew was designed to support the flying boat station at Pembroke Dock, but during the Second World War it developed operational and training roles under the control of No. 15 Group, Coastal Command.

Carew airfield consisted of three concrete runways, two Bellman and two Bessonneau hangars, with the main site located on either side

Photograph of Carew Cheriton Airfield in 1945 taken from a Sunderland
(courtesy D. Brock)

of the A477. The first aircraft to be based at the airfield were Hawker Henleys and Tiger Moths of No. 1 Anti-Aircraft Co-operation Unit. At the outbreak of war several units were attached to the airfield for coastal patrol, including Nos 48 and 217 squadrons equipped with Avro Ansons. In May 1940 members of the Royal Netherlands Naval Air Service who had escaped when the Germans overran Holland arrived in a collection of Fokker T-VIII aircraft. The Dutch Naval personnel became the nuclei of No. 321 squadron. Between July 1940 and April 1941 Carew airfield was bombed five times and therefore several fighter units were based at the airfield for air defence and escort duties. The airfield was transferred to Flying Training Command on 24 July 1942 and again to Technical Training Command on 5 October. The station was officially closed on 24 November 1945.

The site is still evident from the air, with many of the perimeter tracks and runways still visible, but the signs are disappearing fast. A few buildings remain scattered around the airfield.

The re-routed A477 goes through the middle of the technical and domestic site, although the unusual watch tower has been preserved and is now a museum.

Carew's unusual control tower, which has been renovated and turned into a museum

Carew Airfield as seen from the air in 2009

Dale

Land was acquired in 1941 for an airfield to be built near the village of Dale on the northern side of the Milford Haven, opposite the airfield at Angle. It was built as a satellite to Talbenny Airfield and is located just off the B4327, some 12 miles from Haverfordwest.

The airfield became fully operational on 1 June 1942 under the control of No. 19 Group, RAF Coastal Command. It had three concrete and

Fleet Air Arm Mosquito at Dale.
Note the Admiralty control tower in the distance (courtesy V. Summerlee)

Remains of one of the Admiralty's Mainhill hangars

Several wartime buildings still remain at Dale Airfield

An aerial view of Dale Airfield in 2009 (courtesy RCAHMW)

tarmac runways, 3,495 feet, 4,215 feet and 4,785 feet in length. Dispersal points, hangars, workshops and most of the accommodation blocks were located to the north-west of the runways with the main entrance towards the village of Marloes. The first airmen to be based at the airfield was No. 304 (Polish) squadron equipped with Vickers Wellington IC aircraft. The squadron flew maritime reconnaissance patrols in the Bay of Biscay and the Western Approaches until they left in March 1943. In September 1943 the Admiralty exchanged its base at Angle for Dale, which it regarded as better suited for Fleet Air Arm training operations. Under the Fleet Air Arm control an Admiralty control tower and several Mainhill, Main and Pentad hangars were built. It remained under Admiralty control until it closed on 13 December 1947.

Much of the airfield's infrastructure, such as the tower and several of the hangars, has now disappeared; some buildings are still intact but deteriorating very fast. From the air the airfield still looks serviceable. To the south of the airfield was located RAF Kete, a radar station which was absorbed into the Royal Navy Fighter Direction School in 1945 and School of Meteorology in 1946 as *HMS Harrier*. The school closed in 1960 and the base was demolished and returned to farming.

Haroldston West

In 1941, 135 acres were requisitioned from Haroldston Farm and Haroldston Hall for a Relief Landing Ground (RLG) while Withybush Airfield, some five miles away, was being built. Preparation for the landing ground was minimal, with only hedges removed and ditches filled in. The main access to the site was from the Broad Haven road, with Tong Cottage at the edge of the landing area being used by personnel manning the site. Their duty involved placing markers out on the field for incoming aircraft as well as guard duties in a makeshift gun-post.

There is no record of the RLG ever been used, except during the summer of 1942 when a small biplane, probably a Tiger Moth or a Queen Bee, attempted to land. On another occasion one of Carew's Ansons returning from a patrol circled the strip twice but decided it was safer to proceed to Talbenny.

As more airfields became operational in Pembrokeshire, Haroldston West closed in 1943 and the land was returned to its owners.

Haverfordwest / Withybush Airfield

The airfield is situated at Withybush, two miles north of Haverfordwest, just off the A40 to Fishguard. The site was chosen in 1940 and within months land and homes were requisitioned. The airfield was officially opened in November 1942 for No. 17 Group of Coastal Command, but was not fully operational until the following year. The airfield had three runways, the longest being 5,100 feet, with connecting perimeter track with thirty-two dispersal hard stands branching out into surrounding fields. There were two T2 hangars situated near the technical site and administration blocks. The accommodation blocks and other communal sites were situated just off the A40 and scattered in nearby fields.

The first unit to be based at Withybush was No. 3 Operational Training Unit (OTU), equipped with Avro Ansons, Armstrong Whitworth Whitley and Vickers Wellington bombers. Due to limited parking space at the airfield, the unit's 'O' Flight operated from the satellite airfield at Templeton.

In January 1943 Vickers Wellingtons of No. 7 OTU joined the unit to form No. 4 Refresher Flying Unit, but the unit was disbanded in September 1944. Another unit based at the airfield at the time was the General Reconnaissance Aircraft Preparation Pool.

In January 1945 No. 8 OTU (a photo-reconnaissance unit) equipped with thirty Spitfires and Mosquitoes moved to the airfield and stayed there until June. The last units to leave Haverfordwest were Nos 20 and 21 Air Crew Holding Units. The airfield was officially closed in January 1946.

Pembrokeshire County Council acquired the airfield from the Air Ministry in 1952 for civil use, and after lengthy consideration Withybush was chosen as a civil airport covering west Wales. Only minor alterations were required as most of the wartime infrastructure was intact, and on 24 May 1952 Cambrian Airways began a twice daily schedule service to Cardiff (Pengam Moor) using a Dragon Rapide G-AJCL. Swansea was later included in the service which continued until 1955 when Cambrian withdrew from the route.

In 1970 the county council realised the potential of the aerodrome and authorised redevelopment of part of the site. The engineering section was sold and initially used by a number of small businesses; the wartime control tower was refurbished and made into an office. Most of the wartime buildings are occupied by local companies while the one remaining T2 hangar is used by an agricultural firm and on Sundays becomes a market. The main entrance is just off the A40 Fishguard road.

Great effort was made to upgrade facilities at Haverfordwest, and in 2000 a new hangar, a small terminal waiting room and a café was built. A new state of the art control tower became operational in 2004, replacing the control caravan previously used. Another two hangars have since been built, together with parking aprons and an airside apron in front of the terminal. The airfield is now used by air taxi services and a private flying club.

Haverfordwest's wartime control tower, which has been refurbished and is now used as offices

One of the wartime T2 hangars and some buildings still remain at Withybush (Haverfordwest)

Lawrenny Ferry

This small seaplane base was situated four miles from Pembroke on the north shore of the junction of the Cresswell and Carew rivers with the Eastern and Western Cleddau. The site provided a sheltered area for seaplane crew training and was operated by the Royal Navy. It consisted of a single Mains hangar (60 x 70 feet), an 18 foot slipway, three concrete aircraft pens and storage for some 4,800 gallons of fuel. There were no workshops and accommodation for officers and petty officers was provided at Lawrenny Castle. Other ranks were accommodated in two Nissen huts nearby.

The base was commissioned on 1 February 1942 although No. 764 squadron moved here from Pembroke Dock in October 1941. The squadron was equipped with Supermarine Walruses and Seafoxes, towards the end of 1942 supplemented by Chance Vought Sikorsky Kingfisher float-planes. Advance training continued until the squadron was disbanded in November 1943 when the base was put on 'care and maintenance'. It was closed in 1944.

Today very little remains of the base. The slipway still exists and is used by the Lawrenny Yacht Club, but the hangar and Nissen huts were demolished in 1945 and their location is now a site for caravans and holiday chalets.

Manorbier

There were two camps at Manorbier: the Army School of Anti-Aircraft Artillery and the RAF landing strip which supported the school with target towing and pilotless aircraft.

The camp is situated a mile east of Manorbier just off the B4585, some five miles from Tenby. The army camp dates back to 1932 and target towing aircraft of No. 1 Anti-Aircraft Co-operation Unit (AACU) used the field in 1937 during a summer camp training session. By 1939 the temporary huts at both camps had been replaced by permanent buildings. The AACU moved to the new base in May 1939 in support of No. 3 Heavy Anti-Aircraft Practice Camp which had been established at the school. The RAF camp and technical site included a Bellman hangar which was situated to the east of the grass landing area, with additional accommodation in a field leading up to the B4585. The landing area consisted of three landing strips of between about 1,500 feet and 2,400 feet. Towards the end of 1941 there were thirty-five Queen Bees (both manned and unmanned) on the unit's strength. From the outset the landing strip was susceptible to flooding during the autumn and winter months. A novel solution to the problem was the construction of naval hydraulic catapults similar to those installed on Royal Navy cruisers. These catapults were installed on the cliff-tops to launch the Queen Bees over the sea.

The army school was located to the south of the landing strip near the cliff top and consisted of a number of wooden school rooms, accommodation blocks, administration buildings, sick quarters and mess halls. Situated around the cliff tops were various concrete bases for the guns used by the school. During the Cold War the school was upgraded to be capable of utilising the new guided weapons entering service. In the 1960s a new housing estate was built to house the permanent staff at the camp.

As for the landing strip, the pilotless unit was disbanded in March 1946 and the RAF camp closed. The RAF camp has since been completely demolished and the army school is a fraction of its original size. A new helicopter pad has been built and a number of buildings converted for servicing unmanned aerial vehicles (UAVs). The refurbished Bellman hangar is still being used by the school. The guard room, which dates back to 1937, is situated by the main entrance and is still in use.

Pembroke Dock

The flying boat station at Pembroke Dock was officially opened on 1 January 1930. It took advantage of the sheltered inlet of Milford Haven, which had benefited ships of the Royal Navy for centuries.

Initially the base consisted of few wooden huts, a wooden jetty and slipway. There was one Blister type hangar which was demolished when the 'B' type hangar was built. The main alighting area was in Pembroke Reach and had a maximum run of about 4,900 feet. Moorings for the flying boats were adjacent to the base and at Neyland Trot, Burton Trot and Hobbs Point Trot.

During the early 1930s the base was gradually expanded with a new concrete slipway in 1936, an elegant Georgian-style officers' mess, brick built sergeants' and airmen's quarters and new workshops. To accommodate the newer flying boats entering service, two 'B' type hangars were built capable of accommodating three Sunderland flying boats. The eastern hangar was built in 1934 and the western one in 1938. A T2 hangar was built for storage and maintenance in 1943.

Two slipways were built, one being 1,121 feet long with a mechanical winch, while the other was 200 feet with a floating dock nearby. The station was surrounded by a stone wall on the landward side.

The first squadron to be based at Pembroke Dock was No. 210 in May 1931, equipped with Supermarine Southampton flying boats. The squadron remained at the base equipped with various flying boats until July 1940. Most of the squadrons based at Pembroke Dock over the succeeding years had Short Sunderland flying boats, and there were ten Sunderland operational squadrons and one training unit based at Pembroke Dock in the period between 1939 and 1945. Other squadrons were equipped

The elegant guard room and store at the flying boat base main entrance at Pembroke Dock

A Sunderland flying boat on the slipway with the 'B' type hangar behind (courtesy RAFM)

with Consolidated Catalinas. The squadron's patrol area was the Bay of Biscay, the Western Approaches and well out into the Atlantic Ocean.

Another unit based at Pembroke Dock was No. 78 Maintenance Unit which was involved in all major Sunderland servicing and repairs.

In the post-war period the main Sunderland units were Nos 201 and 203 squadrons, and No. 4 OTU (renamed to Operational Conversion Unit) and the Flying Boat Training Squadron with its three Sunderlands.

In the mid 1950s the flying boat was replaced by land-based maritime patrol aircraft and the Sunderland was phased out of service. The last Sunderland was officially withdrawn from RAF service in February 1957

One of two 'B' type hangars which have been refurbished

and No. 208 squadron was disbanded at Pembroke Dock. The station was put on 'care and maintenance' on 31 March 1957 and was officially closed and returned to Admiralty control in 1959, the Admiralty eventually selling the site for redevelopment.

Aerial view of what was Pembroke Dock's flying boat station today

Today most of the site is occupied by a ferry terminal, although the two 'B' type hangars have been renovated and are used by engineering firms. The Georgian officers' mess and the airmen's barrack block were demolished in the 1980s while the sergeants' mess located just inside the elegant main gate was converted into a hotel. The other accommodation site has been developed into a housing estate.

Rudbaxton

Rudbaxton opened as No. 4 Satellite Landing Ground (SLG) on 1 May 1941 for use by No. 38 Maintenance Unit at Llandow. The SLG was situated half a mile north-east of RAF Withybush. Parking space was limited at Llandow, where there was also the constant threat of air raids. The site along the A40 Haverfordwest to Fishguard road consisted of a long, narrow, fairly level strip of ground with clear approaches. Fields adjacent to the strip had hedges removed for access. Also several hides for aircraft were built on the eastern side. Standard buildings for an SLG were a tractor shed, mess room, latrine and watch office, and a private house just off the junction of the A40 and Spittal road was requisitioned as the latter. Most of the aircraft stored at Rudbaxton were Whitleys, Blenheims, Lysanders and Tiger Moths.

Today the tractor shed, mess room and latrine remain and are used by the landowner, while the watch office is once again a private house. Some of the hides are still visible, especially in winter.

Another SLG was planned by No. 38 MU at Picton Park, adjacent to Picton Castle, but was not acquired, although part of the site was used as a landing area for its light observation aircraft.

Remains of the mess room and subsequent tractor shed at Rudbaxton

St Davids

The airfield is situated just off the A487 Haverfordwest to St Davids road a mile from the village of Solva. Approval was given in September 1941 for the acquisition of land near St Davids, to be used to construct an airfield as a satellite for Haverfordwest. Most of the construction took place throughout 1942 and the airfield was opened in September 1943 as part of chain of coastal airfields for RAF Coastal Command.

The airfield had three 150 foot wide tarmac runways, one 5,910 feet long, the second 3,200 feet long and the third 3,570 feet long. Along the perimeter track there were thirty diamond-shaped hard standings in clusters of five. The main site included the technical site, administration, crew huts, and sick quarters, while the control tower was situated to the south. All accommodation quarters and mess rooms were in fields leading off the main site. Two of the airfield's T2 hangars were situated on the main site, while the other was between approaches to two of the runways. Initially it was planned to have four hangars and a number of Blister types, but only three T2 hangars were built, although the base for

A line up of Sea Venoms in front of the control tower at St Davids in 1957

the fourth was laid and was used for additional parking. The station bomb and fuel dumps were located to the north of the airfield. All buildings were either Maycrete or Nissen types.

The first RAF unit to be based at the new airfield No. 517 Meteorological squadron on 26 November 1943, equipped with Handley Page Halifax aircraft. This squadron was joined by another two Halifax squadrons, Nos 58 and 502, in December. The squadrons were involved in meteorological, anti-submarine and convoy patrols. Due to overcrowding, No. 517 squadron moved to Brawdy in February 1944 followed by the other two Halifax squadrons in September. A detachment of Boeing Fortresses II of Nos 206 and 220 squadrons arrived in December 1943.

St Davids airfield was not really suited for Halifax operations due to the alignment of the runways with the prevailing winds, which restricted the aircraft's ability to take off when fully loaded. The usual procedure was to take off from St Davids with a light fuel load and land at nearby Brawdy to top up the fuel tanks. Because of this drawback St Davids airfield was relegated to satellite status and Brawdy became the main base.

Between June and September 1945, Liberators of Nos 53 and 220 squadrons was based at St Davids. On 1 November 1945, the station headquarters and all associated sections moved to Brawdy and the airfield was retained on a care and maintenance basis. St Davids Airfield was taken over by the Admiralty for the Fleet Air Arm on 1 January 1946, as a relief landing ground to Brawdy.

From 1950 the airfield became the base for the Fleet Requirements Unit (FRU) operated by Airwork Limited and equipped with Sea Hornets NF21 and Mosquitoes T33 and eventually Gloster Meteors T7 and DH Sea Venoms in 1957. In 1952 No. 587 RN squadron, equipped with Supermarine Attacker FB 1 aircraft, was also based at the airfield.

The RAF took over the tenure of Brawdy in 1971 and used St Davids as a relief landing ground; at that time one runway was resurfaced and the three T2 hangars were dismantled and rebuilt at Brawdy. When RAF Brawdy closed, St David's airfield was disposed of and most of the land was taken over by the Pembrokeshire Coast National Park Authority. In 2002 the airfield was used as the site for the National Eisteddfod of Wales.

Today the runways, dispersal bays and perimeter track remain, but are breaking up quickly. The few remaining buildings left are used by a local farmer.

Talbenny

Talbenny Airfield is situated on an escarpment overlooking St Bride's Bay, three miles from Dale Airfield. It had three concrete and tarmac runways of 4,800 feet, 3,300 feet and 3,000 feet with a central inter-section, and thirty-six 'frying pan' type hard standings. The technical site was situated on the northern end of one of the runways, while the communal site was off the B4327 Haverfordwest road. The airfield had two T2 hangars built apart, one in the main technical area on the north-east corner and the other on the south-east corner of the airfield.

The airfield officially came into existence on 1 May 1942 under No. 19 Group, RAF Coastal Command with Dale to the south as its satellite station. The first squadron to be stationed at Talbenny was No. 311, a Czech-manned bomber squadron equipped with Vickers Wellington IC aircraft whose duties included anti-submarine patrols and enemy ship-

Talbenny Airfield from the air in 1946

ping strikes in the Bay of Biscay and the Western Approaches. To provide fighter cover for the Wellingtons, detachments of Beaufighters from Nos 235 and 248 squadrons were also based at Talbenny in January/February 1943.

Shipping strikes came to an end in May 1943 and No. 311 squadron left Talbenny and returned to Bomber Command. No. 4 Armament Practice Camp, equipped with Miles Martinets target towing aircraft, was formed at the airfield in April 1943 and remained at Talbenny until September 1945. On 11 October 1943 the airfield was transferred to Transport Command and became an emergency landing ground to which aircraft could be diverted in poor weather conditions. Other units based at Talbenny were No. 16 Flight, and No. 11 Ferry Unit which was made up of Coastal Command Ferry Training and No. 3 Overseas Dispatch Unit. This unit left the airfield in August 1945. The airfield was closed on 23 December 1946.

In the 1950s the airfield's accommodation and other communal buildings were used by the Ministry of Agriculture to accommodate volunteer labourers recruited to help with the harvest on local farms. Most of the airfield's infrastructure, including the hangars, was demolished in the late 1950s and early 1960s. Sections of the runways were also broken up and the land returned to farming, but the airfield layout is still visible from the air. There are still some of the technical site buildings remaining, while the operations block and various buildings on the communal site still stand and are in use today

Templeton

Land was requisitioned near the village of Templeton in 1941 for the construction of an airfield to act as a satellite to Haverfordwest (Withybush). The airfield is wedged between the A4115 and the A4075.

Most of the construction took place during 1942 and the airfield was officially opened in January 1943. It had three concrete and tarmac runways measuring 3,000, 3,300 and 4,800 feet in length. Most of the dispersal pans were situated to the north and west of the runways. The main camp including workshops, training schools, administration, watch office and the sole T2 hangar was located just off the A4115, with No. 1 site on the other side of the road. The airmen and WAAF accommodation sites were dispersed in adjoining fields. The choice of location was questionable as there was a hill situated in the middle of the triangular runway layout which obscured an all-round view.

Initially none of the RAF commands had a requirement for the airfield and construction was temporarily halted, but eventually it was used to ease the acute parking problem at Withybush.

The first unit to be based at Templeton was No. 306 Ferry Training Unit with twenty-three Bristol Beauforts, but in March the unit moved to Northern Ireland. The next unit to move from Withybush (Haverfordwest) was No. 3 Coastal Operational Training Unit (OTU) equipped with Ansons, Wellingtons and a few remaining Whitleys. The OTU remained at Templeton until it was disbanded in January 1944. During the summer months it was often used by Martinets and Spitfires of No. 595 squadron from Aberporth during their towed target glider trials. Between February and June 1945 a small engineering section remained at Templeton to maintain the Spitfires and Mosquitoes of No. 8 OTU at Haverfordwest. When 8 OTU left in June 1945 the station more or less closed but remained under Haverfordwest's control.

The airfield was finally sold in 1960 but was leased back by the Ministry of Defence shortly afterwards and is used as a Dry Training Area for various equipment trials.

Very little remains of the wartime buildings and most of the airfield is obscured by undergrowth.

Templeton as it is today,
all the wartime buildings having been demolished

Appendix

An A to Z of Victorian and later military sites in Pembrokeshire

Amroth to Wiseman's Bridge – This area was used during summer 1943 for Operation Janzen rehearsal for the D-Day landings. Including the construction of a Forward Airfield inland, all evidence was completely removed after the exercise.

Angle Airfield – see chapter 7.

Angle Windmill – During the Second World War the disused 17th-century windmill overlooking Angle Airfield was converted into a defence post with a reinforced concrete floor and machine gun loops.

Angle Point – south of Milford Haven near to the lifeboat station on the cliff top were anti-aircraft machine gun posts.

Bicton (NE of St Ishmaels)- During the Second World War this was the site of heavy and light anti-aircraft batteries with a mixture of 3-inch, 3.7-inch and 40mm Bofor guns.

Bush Camp – used during the First World War as an army camp and during the Second World War by a Barrage Balloon unit.

Brawdy – A Second World War airfield, post-war it was used by the Admiralty, then by the RAF and now by the Army. See chapter 7.

Brunt Farm – Site of a Second World War 3.7-inch mobile heavy anti-aircraft battery.

Bwlch Gwynt, Crymych – a searchlight unit.

Bwlch-y-Defaid, nr **Letterston** – In 1941 a POW camp was built at the site to house mostly Italians. The camp consisted of 8 huts.

Carew Cheriton – A Second World War RAF airfield built on the site of the First World War RNAS Pembroke. See Chapter 7.

Castlemartin – Tank training ranges was established in the 1930s and are still used today.

Cernydd, Maenclochog – A Second World War searchlight unit site.

Chapel Bay Fort – see chapter 5.

Claberston Road district – During the Second World War there were searchlight batteries at Beacon Hill, Upper Haythog, Fenton and Wiston Woods.

Clynderwen House – was taken over as a convalescence centre for American troops.

Dale Airfield – initially a Second World War RAF airfield taken over by the Fleet Air Arm. See chapter 7.

Dale Meadow – this was the site of a large First World War army training camp with hutted accommodation for over 1,000 men.

Deerland Farm – Located north of St Ishmael's near Butterhill was a site of a searchlight battery.

Defensible Barracks – see chapter 5.

Dinas Cross – Site of a Coast Artillery Battery during the Second World War. The battery consisted of 6-inch QF guns and two 3-inch UP rocket launchers. Today it's a caravan site and the observation and command post has been converted into facilities for the holiday camp.

East Blockhouse – see chapters 3 and 5.

Fishguard Bay – a RNAS seaplane base during the First World War. See chapter 6.

Fishguard Fort – see chapters 3 and 5.

Flimston – site of a small civilian/military airfield in 1937/8. The airfield included of three Bessonneau hangars and some wooden buildings. It was mostly used by the army units training at nearby Castlemartin ranges, especially during the summer months.

Garn Fawr – a First World War coast watcher hut, also an ASV (air to surface vessel) radar.

Garnwen, Brynberian – the moorland and surrounding hills were used as a Second World War tank training range.

Geotty Mountains, Rosebush – The location of an army summer camp dating back to 1900.

Great Castle Head – The site of a Second World War light anti-aircraft battery equipped with 3-inch guns.

Gwaun Valley, Mynyddd Gareg Lwyd – a Second World War searchlight battery manned by 77 S/L Regiment, Royal Artillery.

Haroldston – a Relief Landing Ground. See chapter 7.

Hayscastle Cross – site of a radar station. See Chapter ADD.

Hubberston Fort – built between 1860 and 1865. See chapter 5.

Kete – In 1940 RAF Kete was formed as a radar station for tracking low flying aircraft. In 1945 it was taken over by the Admiralty and absorbed into the Royal Navy's Fighter Direction School and later became a School of Meteorology. The station closed in 1960.

Lamphey – During the First World War Windsor Farm was the site of a hutted army camp. In the Second World War it was No. 5 site of RAF Pembroke Dock. Another Second World War site was at Lamphey Court occupied by two companies of the 110th Infantry, 28th US Infantry Division.

Lawrenny Castle – This was a large manor house which during the First World War was a base for an 18-pounder horse-drawn unit. During the Second World War the house was the HQ of No. 4 Light Anti-Aircraft regiment, Royal Marines.

Lawrenny Ferry – A Second World War seaplane station. See chapter 7.

Lawrenny vicinity – Second World War searchlight units were based at Deals Cross, Lawrenny, Newton and Coedcanlas.

Llanion Barracks – site of an army camp dating back to the Crimean War, used during both World Wars. Most of the construction took place during the Second World War. The last regiment based at the barracks was No. 37 Heavy Air Defence Regiment, Royal Artillery in 1967. Today most of the buildings are used as offices.

Llanreath Oil Depot – This was an Admiralty oil storage depot consisting of 17 tanks surrounded by earthworks. In August 1940 they were bombed by German aircraft which destroyed several tanks and caused a fire which burned for three weeks claiming the lives of five firemen. In 1985 the remaining oil tanks were demolished.

Llanreath Wireless Station – This was a First World War Y-Station capable of intercepting German radio transmissions. It remained a wireless station throughout Second World War and is still used by the MOD as a radar station.

Llanrian – There were a number of searchlight units sited in the area: Penlan near Trefin, Abereiddy and Tresaer.

Maesgwynne Farm – On the outskirts of Fishguard was located a large Royal Marine camp. During an air-raid by a lone bomber on 23 September 1941 three personnel were killed.

Milford Docks – Originally built as a naval dockyard on private land. The owner was unwilling to sell the land so the Navy moved to Pembroke Dock. The dock was developed as a commercial port and became a base for a fishing fleet. During the First World War Milford became a minesweeper base for the trawlers pressed into service.

Mynydd Dinas – situated near the village of Dinas was a high frequency/ direction finding station.

Nevern – Located near Trewern was a searchlight battery.

Newton Noyes – Site of a Royal Navy depot for manufacturing and storage of mines dating back to 1930. The complex comprised of a large underground storage space.

North East Gun tower, Pembroke Dock. – see chapter 5.

Paterchurch Battery – see chapter 5.

Pennar Barracks – The barracks were built in 1903 for Royal Engineers to support the submarine mining establishment at nearby Pennar Point. The barracks consisted of workshops, offices, mine store, married quarters and accommodation huts. During the Second World War the site was used by the Royal Navy. The base has since been demolished and is now a housing estate.

Pill Fort – See chapter 5.

Pill Point – A small Balloon station was located at the site during the First World War.

Popton Fort – See chapter 5.

Portclew – Site of a mobile Ant-Aircraft Battery.

Pwllcrochan – Site of a Second World War searchlight unit.

RAF Folly – Situated on the coast between Roch and Nolton was a series of radar aerials built in 1940. The camp's domestic site was located a few miles away at Roch Gate crossroads. Over the years it was updated until the station closed in 1958.

RAF Pembroke Dock – See chapter 7.

RAF St David's – see Chapter 7.

RAF Strumble Head – Location of a radar station. Chain Home Low 1 was at Trenewydd and Chain Home Low 2 was at Treathro.

RNAS Pembroke – A First World War airship station at Milton. See chapter 6.

Rosebush Reservoir – Steel gables were stretched across the lake to deter seaplanes landing. Until recently the concrete anchors could still be seen.

Royal Naval Dock Yard, Pembroke Dock – An 80 acre site protected by high walls and gun towers built in 1814.

Rudbaxton – In 1941 it was the site of a Storage Landing Ground for use by No. 38 Maintenance Unit at Llandow. See chapter 7.

St Botolph – this former mansion near Liddeston was used by the Army during the Second World War to control all Anti-Aircraft batteries in the Milford Haven area.

St Catherine's Fort, Tenby – See chapter 7.

St Daniel's Hill – Site of a heavy Anti-Aircraft battery with its accommodation at Norgan's Hill between Monkton and Maidenwells.

St David's Head – A First World War Submarine Listening Post, a hydrophone station. On Carn Llidi during the Second World War there was a radar station.

St Twynnells – During 1940/41 this was the site of a Home Chain radar station. Post-war it became one of the ROTOR sites during the Cold War period.

Sawdern Point – A single storey brick built night shelter with a concrete flat roof. It was part of the 'Starfish' (SF) night time decoy sites consisting of light and fire located miles from the target to confuse enemy bombers that might be attacking, in this case, Pembroke Dock.

Scoveston Fort – See Chapter 5.

Stackpole Court – During the Second World War it was proposed to be used as a military hospital, but the suggestion was not taken up.

Stack Rock Fort – See chapter 5.

South Hook Fort – See chapter 5.

South West Gun Tower, Pembroke Dock – see chapter 5.

Talbenny – A Second World War airfield. See chapter 7.

Templeton – A Second World War airfield. See chapter 7.

Thorn Island Fort – See chapter 5.

Trecwn – A Royal Naval Armament Depot built in 1938 to store and supply mines and munitions for the Royal Navy. The depot had 58 caverns for storage, connected by a railway line. During the Second World War it was involved in manufacturing 3-inch, 4-inch and 4.5-inch shells. The depot was decommissioned in 1992 and at the moment is awaiting disposal.

Trewarren House – used by Royal Marine light anti-aircraft battery and a HQ for F Troop, 25 Battery, 4 LAA Regiment, whose responsibility was manning the nearby gun batteries.

Twr-y-Felin near Wiston – Site of a Second World War high frequency/ direction finding radio aerial.

Ty-grig, Pant-bach, Rosebush – These were locations of temporary US and British camps prior to the D-Day landings.

Upper Blacknuck, Maenclochog – Site of a mobile Second World War searchlight unit.

Wallaston – An RAF high frequency/direction finding station for moni-toring and plotting lost aircraft and directing them to the nearest airfield.

Warren – RAF Warren was a Second World War radar station. Nearby was 'Z' Battery manned by No. 130 AA Battery, Royal Artillery armed with 2-inch (unrotated projectiles (UP) anti-aircraft rockets.

Watch House Point – Between Monk Haven and Lindsway Bay is the site of Soldier's Rock Coastal Artillery Searchlight Battery with two searchlight units in concrete emplacements and two ex-naval 6-inch breech-loading Mk XII guns. The camp consisted of several concrete and Nissen type buildings.

Watwick – Located north of the West Blockhouse, this was a site of a Second World War anti-aircraft battery for the defence of the Haven against mine-laying aircraft. Nearby in Watwick Bay was the anchor point of the Milford boom defence.

West Pennar – During the Second World War there were four 3.7-inch Mk II anti-aircraft guns in a sandbagged emplacement with a brick built command post. In 1944 the guns were withdrawn to the south of England for defence against the V1 flying bomb. Also there was a single searchlight unit nearby which was bombed and machine gunned during a raid on Pembroke Dock.

Whetstone Hill – Site of a Heavy Anti-Aircraft battery equipped with four 3.7-inch MkII anti-aircraft guns overlooking Gravel Bay. The guns were controlled from a concrete rectangle command post equipped with a mechanical predictor which could calculate the height and speed of an approaching enemy bomber.

Wind Hill – A Second World War searchlight battery consisting of four units with 13 huts and three weapon pits.

Withybush (Haverfordwest) – Second World War airfield, see chapter 7.

Wolfscastle area – There was a searchlight battery at Garn Turne Rocks during the Second World War.

Glossary

Barbette Raised gun position so guns can be fired over the parapet.

Bastion A projecting part of a wall, rampart or fortification.

Battery Guns/cannons grouped together to facilitate better battlefield communication and concentrated fire power.

Boom A chain or cable barrier stretched across a waterway.

Breech-loading In which a shell is loaded into the chamber integral to the rear of the barrel.

Calibre The diameter of the bore of a gun.

Caponier Small, single or double storey structure providing embrasures for cannons and muskets.

Casemates A bomb proof chambers in a structure containing gun positions.

Counterscarp The exterior side of a ditch on the outside of the structure.

Counterscarp gallery Gallery for muskets or light cannons built into the outer face of a ditch.

Embrasure An opening in a wall or parapet through which cannon or muskets were fired.

En-barbette Raised platforms for cannons to be fire over parapets.

Glacis Cleared area usually sloped in front of a fort.

Magazine Fortified room or building in a fort or battery for storing gunpowder and ammunition.

Ravelin A triangular outwork situated in front of a curtain wall.

Rifled-muzzle loading A gun in which the shell or projectile and charge is loaded through the front of the gun (muzzle). The rifle grooves are inside the barrel which causes the projectile to spin in flight giving greater stability.

Scarp An interior wall of a ditch.

Sconce Temporary star-shaped artillery fort of earth and timber, a style that appeared during the Civil War.

Traverse A parapet across a covered way or a location to prevent reverse firing along a work.

Index

Also from Logaston Press

Pembrokeshire: another year, another day
128 pages, 116 colour photographs.
Paperback £12.95   Hardback £20

This volume includes the work of eight local photographers. The photographs are arranged to broadly run from early morning in winter through the soft light of spring, the stronger light of summer and the varied colours of autumn, to conclude with a series of winter sunsets. The subjects include stretches of the county's coastline, historic sites, the Preseli hills, the Gwaun Valley, Tycanol and Pengelli woods and even some below the surface of the sea.

Around & About South-West Wales
by Graham Roberts.   288 pages with 300 b/w photographs   £12.95

Ten road-based tours cover Pembrokeshire, Cardiganshire, Carmarthenshire, parts of Glamorgan and a large part of Powys. Starting from seven different localities the tours cover a range of spectacular scenery, many well and less well known historically or architecturally interesting buildings, several towns, a good handful of villages, many beaches, a clutch of prehistoric sites, gardens open to the public, nature reserves and much besides. Ranging from 25 to 100 miles in distance, each tour contains detailed route information and information about the places en route.

The Story of the Milford Haven Waterway
by Sybil Edwards.   224 pages with over 140 b/w illustrations   £12.95

This book, a major revision of that first published in 2001, focuses on how the Milford Haven waterway has shaped and developed the fortunes of the settlements along its shores, from the arrival of early man through to the present day. Throughout the book the story is interspersed with personal recollections and views to create a feeling of a living waterway that has seen both good times and bad times. Sybil Edwards has been a journalist all her working life.

The Civil War in Pembrokeshire
by Terry John.   192 pages with 35 b/w illustrations   £12.95

This book explores the lives and characters of the three main protagonists, Rowland Laugharne, John Poyer and Rice Powell, and the events of the First and Second Civil Wars with the ebb and flow of march and counter-march, siege and battle. Using many letters and records of the time, Terry John provides a readable account of intense times full of men and women of principle and many a (male) rogue.